# Birnbaum's 2007

Walt Disney World

# Dining Guide

A Complete
Insider's
Guide to
Dining
Disney Style

**THE OFFICIAL GUIDE**

Wendy Lefkon
EDITORIAL DIRECTOR

Jill Safro
EDITOR

Debbie Lofaso
DESIGNER

Lois Spritzer and Pam Brandon
CONTRIBUTING WRITERS

Alexandra Mayes Birnbaum
CONSULTING EDITOR

Jessica Ward
EDITORIAL ASSISTANT

DISNEP EDITIONS
New York

*For Steve Birnbaum, who merely made all of this possible*

ISBN 1-4231-0053-0

Printed in the United States of America

---

**Other 2007 Birnbaum's Official Disney Guides:**

*Disney Cruise Line*
*Disneyland*
*Walt Disney World*
*Walt Disney World For Kids, By Kids*
*Walt Disney World Without Kids*

# A Word From the Editor

It has been said (and sung) that "it's a small world after all." It is not. In fact, Disney's world is so vast (about 47 square miles) and has dining places so plentiful (there are hundreds of them) that picking the right spot to satisfy your group's diverse tastes can be a daunting experience.

It doesn't have to be. We assure you that whatever your palate prefers—simple or sublime, fast food or fine dining—it's being served up somewhere at Walt Disney World. Of course, finding (and reserving) the meal of your dreams can be a challenge. That's where this book comes in. If you're in search of a light snack or a filling lunch, a character breakfast or a champagne brunch—you'll find it described within these pages. You'll also discover rousing dinner shows, theme park favorites, quiet gems off the beaten path, and much more.

Given the popularity of many WDW eateries, booking a table in advance is nearly as important as selecting a venue. Our "WDW reservations" explanation will help you do just that.

Don't forget, you also need to be thinking about what you want to do later in the evening. Please, take your time, and when you're ready to strategize after-dinner entertainment, just flip to our *Clubs and Lounges* chapter. It delivers the scoop on

Downtown Disney (which includes Pleasure Island) and the BoardWalk entertainment zones, as well as compelling spots in the parks and resorts.

Rest assured, a lot of time and calories have gone into the creation of the dining guide you're holding. This is not merely an alphabetical restaurant listing—there are telephone books for that. Our hardy band of editorial gourmands has visited each and every establishment and sampled the fare. If we love a place, you'll know. If we agree that an eatery isn't worth a rave, it won't get one. But our opinions are just that, opinions. The truth is, one reader may see a giant turkey leg as a meal fit for a king, while the same snack leaves another feeling decidedly less regal. We understand that. Our goal is to provide all readers with the information necessary to ensure a successful Disney dining experience.

Chapters in this book are organized by Walt Disney World's parks and resort hotels, with one section focused on eateries within the Downtown Disney entertainment district, another devoted to dinner shows, and one focused on clubs and lounges. We've also included two bonus chapters: the first describes the Disney Dining Plan, and the second reveals some of the most revered and requested recipes in WDW history.

Dining establishments are noted for location, food quality and variety—and ambience. Within each entry there is a price rating and a listing of the meals served. Signature dishes may be listed, but menus (and chefs) do change, so if the braised lamb shank is *the* reason you're headed for a certain restaurant, it's best to call ahead.

If a seven-course gourmet meal is a crucial part of your vacation happiness, you're in luck. If you'd rather enjoy breakfast with Mickey Mouse or have lunch in a castle, you won't be disappointed. It's also possible to dine on couscous in Morocco, stroll to Germany for a knockwurst, to France for quiche, or to the United Kingdom for bangers and mash (don't turn up your nose; it's delicious). In other words, the gastronomic opportunities at Walt Disney World are bountiful, with nearly 6,000 different dishes on its collective menu. From appetizer to dessert, and even a nightcap, we hope this fills the bill.

*Bon appétit!*

# HELPING HANDS

This book was made possible thanks to a tireless team of dedicated diners and behind-the-scenes support. Heartfelt thanks go to Craig Dezern, Rick Sylvain, Linda Warren, Ken Potrock, Darlene Papalini, Laura Simpson, Jeff Titelius, Judi Rosean, and Dave Herbst. Special thanks to Karen Haynes, who has done so much to ensure the accuracy of Birnbaum's Official Walt Disney World Dining Guide.

Kudos to Diane Hodges, Guy Cunningham, and Sue Macy, copy editors extraordinaire. Thanks, also to Erica Warcholak, Nisha Panchal, Janet Castiglione, Monica Mayper, Sharon Krinsky, and Sue Cole for their editorial support and production panache.

Hats off to our "volunteer" tasters: Margaret Verdon, Linda Verdon, Trace Schielzo, Irene Safro, Roy Safro, Joy Safro, and Amy Safro.

Of course, no list of acknowledgments would be complete without our founding editor, Steve Birnbaum, who continues to be an inspiration for us all, as well as Alexandra Mayes Birnbaum, who is both a guiding light and careful reader of every word.

# Table of Contents

## A GUIDE TO THIS GUIDE

This book is a comprehensive guide, with details about each and every eatery on Walt Disney World property. Rather than present you with a book of epic proportions, we've labored to keep the project pocket-sized by combining concise descriptions with handy symbols. Each restaurant entry is preceded by a symbol that indicates whether the establishment is a fast-food spot or a table-service restaurant. We've also indicated whether or not said restaurant is a participant in the Disney Dining Plan (see page 127 for details). Here's a rundown of the symbols:

= Fast Food

= Table Service

= Disney Dining Plan Participant

**B** = Breakfast

**L** = Lunch

**D** = Dinner

**S** = Snack

**$** = Under $15

**$$** = $15–$29

**$$$** = $30–$50

**$$$$** = $51 and up

Prices are based on an average adult meal consisting of a beverage, entrée, and either one appetizer, side order, or dessert (before tax and tip). Note that lunch and breakfast generally cost less.

# How to Book a WDW Table

**T**he guide you are holding will help you select an ideal locale in which to enjoy every Walt Disney World meal. Picking the perfect place, however, is merely step one in the Disney dining experience. We cannot overemphasize the importance of the follow-up step: *booking* it—well in advance. For an explanation of WDW's unique reservations system, turn the page. . . .

# Walt Disney World Reservations

Walt Disney World has reservations about reservations. It seems the traditional system inevitably led to delays, thanks to no-shows and latecomers. As a means of expediting matters, Disney modified the process. Essentially, this means that you arrange to receive priority treatment when it comes to being seated at an agreed upon time. Here's how it works: Call to request a time at a table service eatery; arrive about 10 to 15 minutes before the assigned time and check in; receive the next available table that can accommodate your party. (There may be a wait involved.)

If an eatery accepts reservations, make them. Times can be secured up to 180 days ahead by calling 407-WDW-DINE (939-3463). Hours are 7 A.M. to 10 P.M. If you are unable to book ahead of time, try to make same-day arrangements. Most restaurants will accommodate walk-ins who are willing to wait (just don't arrive starving!).

Disney resorts often have a phone in the lobby area that provides direct contact with the "Dine Line." Simply touch *55—the call is toll-free. From theme park pay phones, touch *88 (also toll-free). Otherwise, call 407-WDW-DINE.

## Hot Tip

*At press time, dining prices for "kids" covered guests ages 3 through 9. Most WDW table-service eateries have special menus just for little ones. Fast-food establishments offer special kid-friendly items, too.*

For same-day arrangements in the Magic Kingdom, go to City Hall; in Epcot, head to Innoventions Plaza; in the Disney-MGM Studios, go to the corner of Hollywood and Sunset; in Animal Kingdom, ask at Guest Relations. Bookings can be made at Downtown Disney Guest Relations. Of course, plans can be made at the restaurants themselves.

Keep in mind that a WDW restaurant reservation is not a traditional reservation. Don't be surprised if you have to wait a while when you arrive at your assigned time. Rest assured, your party will be given the first table that opens up.

## WHAT DO YOU THINK?

No contribution is of greater value to us in preparing the next edition of this book than your comments on what we have written and on your own Walt Disney World dining experiences. Please share your thoughts and insights with us by writing to:

Jill Safro, Editor
Birnbaum's Walt Disney World Dining Guide 2007
Disney Editions
114 Fifth Avenue, 14th Floor
New York, NY 10011

Note that all WDW dinner shows (page 109) must be booked in advance. The Hoop-Dee-Doo Musical Revue, the Spirit of Aloha dinner show, and Mickey's Backyard Barbecue accept requests up to 180 days in advance.

Finally, the Disney dining scene is ever-evolving and procedures tend to change, so we advise calling 407-WDW-DINE to confirm current reservation policies.

## NO RESERVATIONS? NO PROBLEM.

Disney's reservations system was designed to allow for walk-ins (who are willing to wait). That said, some places are easier to gain access to than others. If you want to play it safe, call 407-WDW-DINE from wherever you happen to be and ask about restaurant seating availability. In the meantime, here are a few of our favorite places to pop into without an advance reservation:

• Biergarten (Epcot)
• Big River Grille & Brewing Works (BoardWalk)
• Cap'n Jack's Restaurant (Downtown Disney Marketplace)
• Hollywood Brown Derby (Disney-MGM Studios)
• Le Cellier Steakhouse (Epcot)
• Mama Melrose's Ristorante Italiano (Disney-MGM Studios)
• Palio (Swan resort)
• Plaza Restaurant (Magic Kingdom)
• Rainforest Cafe (Animal Kingdom)
• Yachtsman Steakhouse (Yacht Club)

# Magic Kingdom

**A** lot has changed since Walt Disney World's original theme park opened in 1971. Back then, when it came to quelling hunger pangs, it was pretty much burger or bust. Nowadays, the options are a lot more diverse—with everything from egg rolls to cinnamon rolls, smoked turkey legs to chicken Marsala, clam chowder to coconut fried shrimp. Regardless of your tastes or budget, the seven "lands" in the Magic Kingdom boast a bounty of palate pleasers for the whole family.

# ADVENTURELAND

### 🏃 Aloha Isle

**S** **$**

Switzerland meets Hawaii (hey, this *is* the
Magic Kingdom) at this snack stand next to
the Swiss Family Treehouse. Stop here for all
things pineapple—juice, spears, floats, and
the perennial favorite, the Dole Whip frozen
pineapple soft-serve dessert. This spot has
been around forever—they're definitely
doing something right.

### 🏃 El Pirata y el Perico

**L S** **$–$$** 🍭

Though its name translates to "The Pirate
and the Parrot," you won't find pirates or
parrots at this shady stop across from Pirates
of the Caribbean. Instead, you can munch on
beef empanadas (pastry filled with ground
beef, topped with diced tomatoes, onions,
and salsa), taco salads, tacos, and nachos.
The venue operates seasonally, so it may not
be open during your visit.

### 🏃 Sunshine Tree Terrace

**S** **$**

After your visit to the Enchanted Tiki
Room—Under New Management, you can
take a cool break with some of the most
refreshing snacks in the Magic Kingdom—
slushes and citrus swirls (ice cream swirled
with orange, raspberry, or lemon slush).
Cappuccino, espresso, and soft drinks round
out the menu. A Disney classic, the Sunshine
Tree has been serving chilly treats for as long
as we can remember.

# FANTASYLAND

## 🍴 Cinderella's Royal Table
**B L D** **$$$** 🐭

You don't have to be a prince or a princess to eat like one. At least, not here in the Magic Kingdom. This regal establishment, tucked inside Cinderella Castle, is a high-ceilinged re-creation of a majestic mead hall. It's small as Disney restaurants go, but there's no feeling cramped—thanks to a limited number of tables and towering windows that overlook Fantasyland. It's definitely the most upscale eatery in this kingdom, but for many it's worth every royal penny.

Cinderella welcomes guests into her home for three meals a day, seven days a week—but she's only on hand for breakfast and lunch (though her Fairy Godmother spreads her magic at all meals). Her dinner guests can feast on dishes such as prime rib or pan-seared salmon, plus mashed potatoes and a fresh veggie side. Breakfast and lunch fare tends to be upstaged by Cinderella and friends. The *enormously* popular all-you-can-eat character meals tend to book up the full 180 days ahead, leaving no room for spontaneity. (See page 17 for details on booking.)

The Once Upon a Time Breakfast costs $22 for adults, $12 for children ages 3 through 9; or $32 for adults, $22 for kids including the "Princess Photo Package." (See page 18 for details. The Fairy Tale Lunch costs $24 for adults, $14 for children 3 through 9; with the Princess Photo Package, lunch runs $34 for adults, $23 for kids. Dinner is now a fixed-price affair called Dreams Come True. In addition to a

## Hot Tip

*The Magic Kingdom is a dry kingdom. Guests in search of drinks of a more spirited variety need look no further than beyond the Magic Kingdom's borders. Cocktails are served everywhere else at WDW.*

visit by Fairy Godmother, dinner includes an appetizer, entrée, and dessert. Dinner costs $39.99 for adults, $24.99 for kids. Reservations are downright necessary. Be sure to call exactly *180 days in advance*, first thing in the morning (7 A.M. Eastern Standard Time or earlier), and keep your fingers crossed.

### Enchanted Grove
**S** **$**

What's enchanted about this snack shack is its ability to cool you off with a lemonade, lemon slush, or a strawberry-vanilla ice cream soft-serve swirl. It's on a path that borders Tomorrowland and is easy to miss— so pay attention!

### Mrs. Potts's Cupboard
**S** **$**

Ice cream fans will appreciate this walk-up window near the Many Adventures of Winnie the Pooh. It offers soft-serve cones; hot fudge, strawberry shortcake, and brownie sundaes; plus shakes and floats.

### Pinocchio Village Haus
**L D S** **$-$$**

One of the better spots to target with kids in tow is Pinocchio Village Haus. It's a Small

# TOUGHEST TiCKETS iN TOWN

Cinderella's Royal Table Character Dine is—hands down—the most difficult reservation to secure at Disney World. Why? For starters, Cinderella is one popular princess. And there's the allure of dining in the castle—the most famous landmark in the world's most popular theme park. Add to that the fact that the restaurant is small (122 seats) and you end up with a supply-and-demand issue.

The good news is, thanks to a change in policy and the addition of a princess-hosted lunch, it's gotten slightly less impossible to snag a seat at Cinderella's table. Potential guests still reserve by calling 407-939-3463 (WDW-DINE) 180 days ahead, but now they must pay for the meal at the same time the reservation is booked. There is no charge for infants, but they must be included in the reservation.

Expect your credit card to be charged immediately upon making the reservation. Cancellations or changes must be made at least 24 hours prior to the reservation to receive a refund. The only one who can change or cancel a reservation is the one whose name is on the card.

Reservations cannot be transferred, and the lead name may not change.

Guests must present the credit card that was used to book the reservation, but may charge the meal to a different card or the Disney Dining plan.

*Continued on page 18*

World's next-door neighbor seems small from the outside, but don't be fooled by appearances: there's a half dozen dining rooms inside. The most popular room boasts picture windows that overlook the It's a Small World loading area. It's fun to watch the boats bob by as you munch on lunch. It's a good place to take the kids (or picky eaters) for lunch, dinner, or snacks. They offer pizza, sandwiches, salads, and soft drinks, too. Note that this is a popular

**Continued from page 17**

If your vacation package includes meals, you'll still have to make a reservation with a credit card. Make sure you tell the fine folks at WDW-DINE all about your package, including the confirmation number.

Finally, a word about the Photo Package. If purchased, a Disney cast member will snap a photo of your entire party inside the Castle lobby. By the end of your meal, you'll receive a package including four 4" by 6" prints and one 6" by 8" print of your group, plus one 6" by 8" print of Cinderella Castle. Note that the photo package must be purchased for everybody who actually poses for the picture.

Whew! That's a lot of work for one little dining experience. Is it really worth it? Judging by the scads of smiles we see day in and day out, we have to say yes. Breaking bread with Cinderella is, for many, a memory of a lifetime.

## Hot Tip

*The hours from 11 A.M. to 2 P.M., and again from about 5 P.M. to 7 P.M., are mealtime rush hours in the Magic Kingdom. Try to eat earlier or later whenever possible.*

destination in a bustling neighborhood, so you may want to go a little before or after traditional mealtime rush hours.

### Scuttle's Landing

**S** **$**

This snack stand near Dumbo the Flying Elephant serves up frozen carbonated beverages and soft drinks. The frozen treat is simple, but satisfying—especially if the weather's warm and you find yourself thinking "nothing would hit the spot like some syrupy, Technicolor ice." Kids love it.

# FRONTIERLAND

### Pecos Bill Cafe

**L D S** **$-$$** 🐭

Pecos Bill—an "oldie but goody"— has been feeding hungry cowpokes for more than three decades. The look has changed a bit over time —talking animal heads Buff, Melvin, and Max are gone, and they added an indoor courtyard dining room—but the reliable quality of the burgers and fries remains. Cheeseburgers, sandwiches, chili, salads, and french fries are the staples. (If you'd rather skip the fries, ask for the à la carte version or for a carrot substitute.)

What sets this spot apart from other burger establishments? Two words: fixin's bar. It's chock-full of items with which to garnish your meal. Among them: fresh lettuce and tomato, sautéed mushrooms and onions, and warm, gooey cheese sauce.

The lines grow long during mealtimes. Resist the urge to jump on the first queue you hit and head toward a cashier that's farther from the entrance. The line may be shorter. This is one of the most popular fast-food restaurants in the Magic Kingdom—it's high on our list of favorites, too.

# LIBERTY SQUARE

### Columbia Harbour House
**D S** **$-$$** ♥

Few would expect such an elegant setting in which to snack on chicken strips, chili, tuna and vegetarian sandwiches, fried fish, or New England clam chowder (no longer served in a bread bowl, but still popular), but Disney has done this fast-food emporium up in style—complete with antiques, model ships, harpoons, nautical instruments, and even lace tieback curtains. Cozy is the operative word here—try to snag a window table. Whether it's lunch or dinner, this is a charming stop. In addition to the chowder, we stand by the vegetarian sandwich.

### Liberty Tree Tavern
**D** **$$$** ♥

Step back in time at this early American tavern where the decor has a tendency to outdazzle the fare. Here, the wallpaper looks as if it might have come from Colonial Williamsburg; the curtains hang from cloth loops, and the rooms are filled with mementos that might have been found in the homes of Thomas Jefferson, George Washington, and Ben Franklin. Appropriately enough, the restaurant is located across from the Hall of Presidents attraction.

The lunch menu includes fish, pot roast, turkey, clam chowder, sandwiches, and soups. Dinner is an all-you-can-eat affair— salad, roast turkey, flank steak, pork chops, and macaroni and cheese to name a few items—served family style and hosted by Disney characters. The cost for dinner is $27.99 for adults, $12.99 for children ages 3 through 9. *Desserts and specialty beverages are not included.* Despite the tavern motif, no alcohol is served (this kingdom is not only magic, it's dry). The restaurant is hosted by Stouffer's (expect a preponderance of their products). Reservations are suggested.

## Sleepy Hollow

S $

Often missed by guests rushing toward the Haunted Mansion or other Magic Kingdom hot spots, this underappreciated dessert window has a lot to offer: ice-cream cookie

---

# Hot Tip

*To avoid lines, eat lunch or dinner at a Magic Kingdom restaurant that takes reservations—Tony's Town Square, Crystal Palace, Plaza Restaurant, Liberty Tree Tavern, or Cinderella's Royal Table. Know that you may have to wait a few minutes once you arrive at the eatery.*

---

sandwiches, fresh-baked cookies, funnel cakes, caramel corn, and more are the sweets for sale here. It's located in the Hall of Presidents neighborhood near the Liberty Square bridge. Eat on the adjacent brick patio and you'll get a stunning view of Cinderella Castle at no extra charge.

# MAIN STREET, U.S.A.

### Casey's Corner
**L D S** $ 

Casey's is a grand slam for baseball fans—and those who just happen to love the food associated with America's pastime: big ole hot dogs and crunchy fries. This old-fashioned red-and-white quick stop is on the west side of Main Street (adjacent to Crystal Palace). Tables spill out onto the sidewalk, where a ragtime pianist often tickles the ivories. There's a back room with a table or two, plus bleacher seating and constant screenings of sports-themed animated shorts. The bill of fare retains the mood—jumbo hot dogs, corn dog nuggets, fries, brownies, and soft drinks. You gotta love a place that supplies free cheese sauce and malt vinegar for your fries. It's a popular spot for a late-night snack, and a Magic Kingdom classic.

### Crystal Palace
**B L D** $$-$$$ 

A landmark of sorts, this restaurant—one of the prettiest in the Magic Kingdom—could be a Victorian garden if not for the walls and ceiling. The airy atmosphere provides a

## EARS TO YOU!

As if Mickey Mouse weren't already a sweet character, the folks at the Main Street Confectionery have made him even sweeter. Here you can get Mickey-shaped cookies, lollipops, crispie treats, candy-coated pretzels, and more. Elsewhere, you can snack on Mickey ice-cream bars. They're easy to find and colossally popular. Guests gobble up more than three million of them each year.

pleasant escape from the crowds on Main Street, and the all-you-can-eat buffet is a bountiful—if not terribly creative—spread. Its main attraction is its character, make that *characters*: Winnie the Pooh and friends mingle with guests all day long.

Breakfast features a variety of hot and cold breakfasty items, including omelets, fresh fruits, cereals, and such. The midday meal includes a salad bar, deli bar, pasta dishes, chicken, and fish. Dinner offers more of the same: chicken, pastas, fish, carved meats, and more. Kids love the ice-cream sundae bar (set up for lunch and dinner), as well as the pint-sized and kid-appetite-appropriate section of the buffet.

Located at the end of Main Street, U.S.A. (heading toward Adventureland), the "palace" takes its architectural cues from similar structures that once stood in New York and London's Hyde Park, and from San Francisco's Conservatory of Flowers in Golden Gate Park. There's a Victorian-style indoor garden complete with flowers; tables look out on flower beds, and four topiaries—Pooh, Tigger, Eeyore, and Piglet—greet guests at the entrance.

Cost for breakfast is $18.99 for adults and $8.99 for children ages 3 through 9; lunch is $20.99 for adults, $11.99 for children; dinner is $27.99 for adults, $10.99 for children. Reservations are suggested.

## 🏃 Main Street Bake Shop

**B L S** **$** 🐭

Ever popular, always crowded, this old-fashioned bakery gives off a heavenly aroma and delivers with pastries, pies, sandwiches, and cookies. It's possible to get a quick breakfast, here, too—from bagels to warm cinnamon rolls. The built-to-order ice-cream-cookie sandwiches and the chocolate-chunk cookies are popular indulgences. We recommend the coffee smoothies. The nice surprise is that you can also get yogurt, granola, fresh fruit, and other dry cereal—that is, if your willpower holds out.

## Hot Tip

*Is the Magic Kingdom open late today? If so, consider taking the monorail or a water taxi to the Contemporary, Polynesian, Grand Floridian, or Wilderness Lodge to have an early dinner, and then return to finish the day at the Magic Kingdom. Remember to keep your ticket for re-entry to the park. Transportation (monorail and water taxi) generally runs for one to two hours after the park closes for the day.*

### 🍦 Plaza Ice Cream Parlor

`S` `$`

This nirvana for ice-cream lovers boasts the Magic Kingdom's largest variety of hand-dipped ice-cream flavors, including "no sugar added" varieties. It's great for a before-the-parade or on-the-way-out-of-the-park nosh. To keep things moving, choose your flavors and desired number of scoops before you jump on line.

### 🍽 Plaza Restaurant

`L` `D` `S` `$$` 🐭

Not to be confused with the Plaza Ice Cream Parlor, this place also boasts ice cream as the specialty of the house. Oh wait, that is confusing! Here's how to differentiate: the Ice Cream Parlor is a counter-service, cones-and-cups-only establishment. The Plaza is a table service, you-name-a-way-to-serve-ice-cream-and-they-probably-do-it establishment. Expect heaping sundaes, milk shakes, floats, and more. Also on the menu is a small selection of hot and cold sandwiches, salads, and burgers.

The charming atmosphere and the satisfying fare combine for a top-notch experience. Reservations are suggested.

### 🍽 Tony's Town Square

`L` `D` `$$$` 🐭

Here it's possible to savor a fine view of Town Square while you bite into Italian specialties—pizzas, Caesar salad, sandwiches, and lots of pasta. At dinnertime, the menu features chicken Florentine (one of our favorites), grilled steaks, and spaghetti, along with a variety of daily specials. Top it

## TALKIN' TURKEY

Smoked turkey legs, that is. There's something barbarically compelling about gnawing on one of these popular mega-snacks. If you've had one, you know they're pretty good. Here are some things you may not know about these giant drumsticks:

• Each one weighs about 1½ pounds.
• Disney guests gobble up more than 1½ million of them every year.
• The turkeys that once belonged to these legs weighed 40 to 50 pounds.
• They can be purchased at a cart in the Magic Kingdom's Frontierland and at the Lunching Pad at Rockettower Plaza in Tomorrowland.
• They cost about $7 a pop.

off with an Italian sweet and perhaps a cup of espresso or cappuccino.

If you time it right, you can fold your napkin, pay the check, and wander out onto Main Street and enjoy the fireworks from one of the best vantage points in the Magic Kingdom. Reservations are suggested.

## Hot Tip

*In the mood for a picnic? There is a small area in which to brown-bag it at the Transportation and Ticket Center. It's a handy way to save a little money or to simply enjoy a light snack on the go.*

# TOMORROWLAND

##  Auntie Gravity's Galactic Goodies

**S** | **$**

Ice cream may not seem futuristic, but chances are it'll be around at least another gazillion years, give or take. This timeless treat is one of the items served by this no-frills snack spot. Located across from the Tomorrowland Indy Speedway (between Merchant of Venus and Mickey's Star Traders), Auntie Gravity's also offers up smoothies, soft-serve ice cream, frozen yogurt, sundaes, floats, and fruit cups. There's not much atmosphere in this corner of the galaxy, but the goodies are satisfying.

## Cosmic Ray's Starlight Cafe

**L D S** | **$–$$** | 🐭

As big as all outdoors (not necessarily a plus), this is the largest fast-food spot in the Magic Kingdom. Located directly across from the Tomorrowland Indy Speedway, it's really more like several fast-food spots in one. There are three separate stations, with a different menu offered at each.

The variety is good, but you need to wait in more than one line if you want food from two or three sections. Choose from Bay 1 for rotisserie chicken, barbecue ribs, and chicken sandwiches; Bay 2 for cheeseburgers, vegetarian burgers, and hot dogs; and Bay 3 for soups, salads, sandwiches, and wraps. An Audio-Animatronics lounge singer, Sunny Eclipse, entertains throughout the day.

**Note:** Cosmic Ray's Starlight Cafe offers a small number of kosher menu selections.

## SPECIAL REQUESTS

Watching your salt intake? Find lactose intolerable? Disney World restaurants can accommodate many special dietary requirements (vegetarian, low-sodium, lactose-free, and kosher meals, for example) if requests are made at least 24 hours in advance. Make your personal needs known when you make your restaurant reservations by calling 407-WDW-DINE (939-3463). Be sure to confirm your reservation and special request 24 hours before you arrive. Kosher meals must be reserved with a credit card and require 24 hours for cancellations.

### Lunching Pad at Rockettower Plaza

**S** **$-$$**

If it's just a snack you're after, stop at the base of the Astro Orbiter in Tomorrowland plaza for some character cookies, frozen soda slushes, soft drinks—and even smoked turkey legs (for some, these are substantial enough to comprise a whole meal).

### Tomorrowland Terrace Noodle Station

**L D S** **$-$$**

Offering pleasant views (Cinderella Castle, a topiary sea serpent, graceful willow trees), this retro-futuristic spot on the edge of Tomorrowland serves noodle bowls, stir-fry selections, egg rolls, Asian-style salads, and soft drinks. Operates seasonally.

# Epcot

**T**he eclectic, international lineup of fare offered here threatens to over-shadow the attractions themselves. With no fewer than 11 different countries represented in the World Showcase section of the park, Epcot provides guests with the opportunity to eat their way around the world without leaving Central Florida. Less ambitious diners will likely have their taste needs met, too—there's a bountiful food court in Epcot's Future World, as well as a smattering of simple yet satiating snack spots.

# FUTURE WORLD

EPCOT

## Coral Reef (The Seas)

**L D** **$$$** ♥

This water-themed restaurant is all about nibbling on creatively prepared fish under the watchful eyes of their brethren. The restaurant is decorated in cool greens and blues to complement its surroundings, and every table has a panoramic view of the living coral reef; some are right up against the glass. (Don't worry: you're not actually eating Epcot residents—Disney's catches come fresh from fishing boats in the Atlantic each day.) Menu items run the gamut from a bounty of fresh fish and shellfish, including shrimp, mahimahi, catfish, and salmon—prepared in a number of ways—to grilled New York Strip and pan-seared chicken breast for those who are satisfied simply spying on the fish. And save room for the "white wave" dessert. Reservations are suggested.

## Electric Umbrella (Innoventions Plaza)

**B L D S** **$-$$** ♥

This large locale is decorated in shades of blue, mauve, and magenta. The menu's not imaginative, but the restaurant is a good bet when the weather is temperate enough to allow dining at the tables on the terrace outside—or when bound for World Showcase with finicky eaters in tow. (There are indoor tables, too.) Offerings include burgers, chicken strips, tossed salads, and assorted sandwiches. Beer and soft drinks are also available. Kids enjoy the simple fare here.

# HOLIDAY HOOPLA

During the Christmas holiday season, Epcot's World Showcase hosts a special Candlelight Processional. The show features a stirring choral concert and a reading by a celebrity narrator. The event is free (with park admission), but the general admission seating fills up as early as two hours before showtime. Rather than wait in line, we prefer to book a dinner package—one that combines dinner at a World Showcase restaurant and guaranteed seating at the Processional. For information, call 407-934-7639.

## Fountain View Espresso and Bakery (Innoventions Plaza)
**B S** **$-$$**

Leave your calorie counter at home. Fresh-baked goods and yummy desserts—such as croissants, cheesecake, and more—can be found at this pleasant spot across from the Fountain of Nations. Espresso, cappuccino, and smoothies are among the assorted beverages available here. The coffee, as served in most of WDW, is Nescafé.

## Garden Grill (The Land)
**L D** **$$-$$$**

Guests are often so distracted by the sights and the jovial hosts (Chip, Dale, and friends) that they don't realize the restaurant is actually moving. As the restaurant revolves, and it does so quite slowly, tables drift past various dioramic scenes (which are part of the attraction Living With the Land). Among the nature scenes that may be served with dinner are a thunderstorm, sandstorm, prairie, and rain forest. The scenes were designed with diners in mind and provide you with a peek into a farmhouse window that's out of viewing range of the waterborne passengers.

Chip and Dale (who may be joined by Mickey Mouse and Pluto) host two character meals here each day. Lunch and dinner menus feature rotisserie meats, fresh vegetables (some of which are actually grown inside The Land pavilion!), and a small selection of desserts. There is a separate kids' menu. For adults, the cost is $20.99 for lunch, $27.99 for dinner. Kids pay $11.99 for lunch and $12.99 for dinner. Beverages and dessert (be sure to try the "worms in dirt") are included. Meals are served family style (unlimited, communal platters for the table). Reservations are suggested.

The restaurant moves in a circle. It's imperceptible to most, but if you are highly sensitive to motion it may be best to dine in a more stationary environment.

### Sunshine Seasons (The Land)

**B L D S** $–$$

It's the closest thing to a mall food court you'll find in a Disney World park, but a bit more hectic. Located near the entrance to Soarin' on the pavilion's lower level, this is an ideal destination for parties who can't quite agree on any one type of fare—there's bound to be something for everyone. Tables are scattered in several areas, beneath colorful hot-air balloons. Scouting out a table can be a challenge during peak mealtimes. (There's also quite a bit of pedestrian congestion, thanks to the enormous popularity of Soarin', the attraction located next to the dining area.)

**The Sandwich Board** offers a variety of sandwiches, including Black Forest ham and salami grinders and a roasted vegetable Cuban sandwich. The **Bakery**'s desserts include "Cinderella pumpkin cheesecake," brownies, and ice cream. There is also a "grab and go" section for guests in a hurry. Among the items to choose from are sushi, fruit and cheese, salads, and snack foods. **Grill Shop** offers rotisserie chicken, grilled salmon, and ancho-rubbed rotisserie beef chimchurri served on flat bread with tabbouleh and greens. **Soup and Salad Shop** serves the likes of roasted beet and goat cheese salads and seared tuna salad with sesame rice wine dressing. There is a selection of soups, too. Finally, the **Wok Shop** has Mongolian beef with jasmine rice and noodle bowls (including one of the vegetarian variety).

A word of advice: It's a good idea to split up your party and stand on several lines at once. That'll increase your chances of actually eating together. Before you do so, select a table. That way, everyone in the party will know where to meet after they forage.

## Hot Tip

*Try to fit meals in during a Fastpass window. In other words, go to your favorite attraction, get your Fastpass assignment (a time at which you can return and experience the attraction without standing in a long line), and head to an eatery while the time ticks away.*

# WORLD SHOWCASE

## 🍽 Akershus Royal Banquet Hall (Norway)

**B L D** $$–$$$ 🐭

At Epcot's castlelike Akershus, guests are treated to authentic Norwegian cuisine. This is your chance to sample well-prepared signature dishes that rarely make their way into theme parks. Try a family-style sampling of the Norwegian *koldtbord*, featuring smoked salmon and seafood, authentic Norwegian cheeses, and chilled salads, followed by one of the ever-changing lineups of Norwegian-inspired entrées, including seafood, beef, and poultry selections. If it's offered, and you are so inclined, try the *aquavit* (translated to "water of life," it's a potato vodka flavored with caraway seeds). The kids' menu offers grilled chicken, cheese ravioli, pasta with meatballs, and hot dogs. Dessert is included, as are soft drinks. Don't be daunted by the odd-sounding names of some dishes; servers will explain the offerings.

If you can't get a reservation for the Once Upon a Time princess breakfast in Cinderella Castle, know that this restaurant offers an excellent alternative—and it's easier to snag a table. The Princess Storybook dining takes place here daily (breakfast, lunch, and dinner). While guests enjoy the all-you-can-eat fare, Disney princesses wander about and mingle. Belle, Jasmine, Snow White, Sleeping Beauty, and even Mulan have made appearances. Note that the character appearance schedule varies. Reservations must be made with a credit card. Changes and cancellations must be made at least 48 hours ahead to avoid a $10 per adult, $5 per child charge.

## 🍽 Biergarten (Germany)
**L D** **$$–$$$** 🐭

Year in and year out, this place makes us
happy. It's a reasonably priced, all-you-can-
eat buffet of traditional German cuisine set
in a charming courtyard. Adding to the fun
are communal tables and live entertainment
(at lunch and dinner). It's pretty much
Oktoberfest year-round.

The hearty, varied buffet features a
selection of sausages, rotisserie chicken,
spaetzle, chicken schnitzel, potato salad,
cucumber salad, and many other German
specialties. Wash it all down with soft
drinks, German wine, or a stein of beer
(suds purists may grouse at the limited
selection of beer). Among the dessert
options is a tasty apple strudel.

The entertainment consists of occasional
appearances by traditional Bavarian musicians—each clad in lederhosen or dirndl—
who play accordions, cowbells, a musical
saw, and a harplike stringed instrument
known as the "wooden laughter." Perform-
ances take place at scheduled times in the
dining room. Diners are usually invited to
join the fun on the dance floor. Because
entertainment is intermittent, there's plenty
of time to enjoy the pleasant setting.
Reservations highly recommended, particularly during peak seasons (book early).

## 🍽 Bistro de Paris (France)
**D** **$$$$**

This intimate bistro—one flight above Les
Chefs de France—puts on romantic airs
rather than the usual bustle. The elegant
decor, with its evocative interplay of brass

sconces, milk-glass chandeliers, mirrors, and leaded glass, is convincingly French. And, if you're one of the lucky few who arrive as a window-side table opens up, you'll be treated to a rather unique view of World Showcase.

The traditional upscale bistro menu (created by the same trio of French chefs responsible for the fare at Les Chefs de France; see page 38) features such robust "preludes" as a medley of escargot, frog legs, and *fois gras*. The brief entrée menu includes a double-cut white veal chop, beef tenderloin, and bouillabaisse. This is hearty dining, so you might want to stroll around the promenade to walk off your meal—and your chocolate soufflé. The impressive wine list is *très* French. Reservations are suggested.

## Boulangerie Patisserie (France)

**S  S-$$  ♥**

For some, a visit to Epcot is incomplete without stopping by this ever-popular pastry shop, tucked toward the back of the France pavilion. Crowds are forever lining up to consume the flaky croissants, eclairs, fruit tarts, and chocolate mousse. (We enjoy the sweet temptation aptly known as the Marvelous.) Kronenbourg beer and French wines are also offered.

The treats are served under the management of the stellar trio of chefs—Paul Bocuse, Roger Vergé, and Gaston Lenôtre—who operate the popular Les Chefs de France restaurant not far away. This has become a favorite snacking stop among Epcot veterans. Your best bet is to stop here as soon as World Showcase opens or during Illumi-Nations, the nightly fireworks show (though you can't see the fireworks from here).

### 🏃 Cantina de San Angel (Mexico)
**L D S** $-$$ 🐭

Located along the World Showcase Promenade, just outside the entrance to Mexico's pyramid, this stand serves beef-filled soft tortillas (better than the tacos); tacos al carbón, flour tortillas filled with grilled chicken strips, onions, and peppers, served with refried beans and salsa; and churros (fried dough rolled in cinnamon and sugar). Beer and margaritas are available. (The food here can be underwhelming.)

### 🏃 Cool Post (between Germany and China)
**S** $ 🐭

As its name suggests, this place specializes in all things cool: frozen yogurt, ice cream, and soft drinks. Located between the Germany and China pavilions, it features a constant spritz of water. Not enough to soak you, but certainly enough to cool you off.

### 🏃 Harry Ramsden's Yorkshire Fish Shop (United Kingdom)
**S** $ 🐭

A perfect choice for a quick snack or a light lunch, this stand offers fish-and-chips. (Don't forget the malt vinegar.)

### 🏃 Kringla Bakeri og Kafe (Norway)
**L D S** $-$$ 🐭

This spot serves *kringles,* sweet candied pretzels reserved for special occasions in

Norway; *vaflers,* heart-shaped waffles topped with powdered sugar and jam; *kransekake,* almond-pastry sticks; and *smørbrøds,* open-face sandwiches of smoked salmon, roast beef, or turkey. There are no seats inside, but you can eat in the small, shaded outdoor eating area.

EPCOT

## Le Cellier Steakhouse (Canada)
**L D** **$$–$$$** ❤

We love retreating to this peaceful wine cellar–like spot, a favorite place for a hearty yet bearably priced meal. It may seem a bit dungeony to some critics, but we like that; you really feel as though you're inside a wine cellar. The restaurant, which is on the lowest level of the Canada pavilion, has low ceilings, lantern light, and stone walls, all of which contribute to the atmosphere.

There's a full menu of tempting Canadian foods, with steak sandwiches and salads, and Cheddar cheese soup (this is a house specialty) available for lunch. Canadian Alberta beef adds to the offerings at dinner. Excellent maple-glazed salmon and rosemary garlic-seared chicken and pasta dishes round out the selection of entrées. For dessert, try the classic (and sinfully sensational) crème brûlée or chocolate cake. Microbrews from Quebec, Canadian lagers, and Inniskillin wine are served. Reservations are suggested.

## Les Chefs de France (France)
**L D** **$$$–$$$$** ❤

"Bright lights, big dining room" describes this airy establishment. With three of France's best chefs—Paul Bocuse, Roger

**38** B *breakfast* L *lunch* D *dinner* S *snacks*

Vergé, and pastry guru Gaston Lenôtre—keeping tabs on this nouvelle French kitchen, the results are consistently rewarding. Their menu features fresh ingredients readily available from Florida purveyors, though the restaurant imports as many key ingredients from France as possible.

The offerings are decidedly French, but the foundation of the menu is nouvelle cuisine, which involves lighter sauces using less cream and butter than in classic French cooking. Menu items include seared tuna and baked, stuffed cod. Soups and appetizers, such as onion soup and escargot, are all-day

## FOOD AND WINE FESTIVAL

Once a year, Epcot's already-hopping dining scene expands exponentially in what's known as the International Food and Wine Festival. The event, which runs through much of October and into November, is a celebration of the flavors of dozens of nations. Those countries without permanent stations at World Showcase set up temporary displays from which authentic samples of food and wine are sold. The samples generally range in price from about a dollar to about $6. It's possible to eat and drink your way around the world for about the same price as some table-service restaurants.

The festival also features demonstrations from top chefs as well as wine and cooking seminars. For dates and specifics, visit www.disneyworld.com or call 407-824-4321.

staples. Apple tart, chocolate crêpes, peach melba, and chocolate mousse cake are dessert specialties. Wine pairings are suggested from a modest (though well-rounded) list.

This can be one of the most expensive of all World Showcase restaurants. Still, given its continued popularity, many guests believe it's worth the splurge. Reservations are suggested. (Book early.)

## Liberty Inn
## (The American Adventure)

**L D S** $-$$ 🍴

While it may seem like the flavors of the United States get short shrift when it comes to representation at Epcot, that's not the case here. True, there's no table-service restaurant at World Showcase, though the Garden Grill over in Future World proudly serves up platters of Americana. On the international side of the park, Liberty Inn dishes out helpings of what many have come to think of as American food: burgers, hot dogs, and fries. Also on the menu are salads, barbecue pork, turkey, and chicken sandwiches, apple cobbler, and cookies. Located on the left side of the American Adventure pavilion, this is a good choice for children, as well as guests in need of a burger fix.

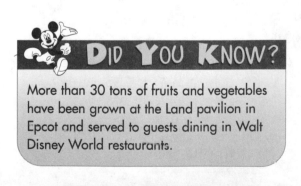

## DID YOU KNOW?

More than 30 tons of fruits and vegetables have been grown at the Land pavilion in Epcot and served to guests dining in Walt Disney World restaurants.

## PLAY WITH YOUR FOOD

Remember when squishing gooey peanut butter through your fingers was a delightfully visceral experience? Well, throw in some marshmallows and chocolate sprinkles and you have a dessert fit for a king—or, at least, for a kid. It's not as gross as it sounds. In fact, this creative confection is one of the most popular of the "interactive desserts" that grace the menus of many Walt Disney World restaurants.

Another example: young diners at Epcot's Le Cellier Steakhouse have changed chocolate mousse into "moose" by adding faces and antlers. Note that interactive desserts aren't offered everywhere and are subject to change.

### 🍽️ L'Originale Alfredo di Roma Ristorante (Italy)
**L D** **$$$** 🐭

Adorned with massive murals that evoke the Italian countryside, this restaurant inspires a "when in Rome" frame of mind from the outset. You suddenly hear an Italian grandma's voice in your head, urging you to "mangia." But do you go with the specialty of the house, the decadently rich fettuccine Alfredo? Or maybe lasagna is more to your liking? It's hard to go wrong at Alfredo's, as fresh pasta is made on the premises (you may get to watch this process near the restaurant's entrance), and Italian wines are in ready supply. There are also a number of less familiar Italian preparations involving chicken, steak, seafood, and veal. It can be a bit pricey, but the restaurant is a perennial guest favorite.

At lunchtime, it's also possible to order pizza. For dessert, choose from specialties such as tiramisu, cannoli, panna cotta, or gelato. This restaurant is at once romantic and festive (occasionally raucous); strolling musicians may enhance the experience. reservations are suggested.

## Lotus Blossom Cafe (China)
**L D S** **$-$$**

The fare may not live up to the splendor of the rest of this pavilion (the film, *Reflections of China*, is quite stirring), but if you crave a quick Chinese food fix, this place, adjacent to Yong Feng Shangdian shopping gallery in the China pavilion, offers orange chicken, rice bowls, salad with peanut dressing, egg rolls, and soup. There is a covered outdoor seating area nearby.

## Marrakesh (Morocco)
**L D S** **$$-$$$**

It's not every day that you can slip into an exquisitely tiled Moroccan palace and expect to be entertained by belly dancers and musicians as you polish off a sampler plate of Moroccan cuisine; even the waiters are dressed in traditional Moroccan costumes. Want to know how authentic this place is? The king of Morocco sent craftspeople to Epcot to make sure they were creating a real Moroccan atmosphere—*and* the king's former chef *works* here. Specialties include roast lamb, chicken brochette, beef shish kebob, and couscous (steamed semolina served with

your choice of lamb, chicken, or vegetables).
Want to experience all of it? Sampler platters
are also available. Reservations are suggested,
but it's often possible to walk up and get in
without much of a wait.

## 🍴 Mitsukoshi (Japan)
**L D** **$$$** 🍭

Within the Mitsukoshi complex (which is
named for and run by the Japanese company
of the same name), there are two options:

**Tempura Kiku** occupies a small, rather
dark corner of the Mitsukoshi building. The
decor may be on the drab side, but the food's
first-rate—as is the view of World Showcase
lagoon (from window tables). If you're in
the mood for sushi, sashimi, or tempura
(batter-dipped, deep-fried chicken, beef,
seafood, and vegetables), head here. It's also
possible to munch on *edamame* (steamed
soybeans) and indulge in sake and Japanese
beer, among other cocktails. There may be a
wait for dinner, but it's usually less of a wait
than at neighboring restaurants. Reservations
are not available here, but we've never had
to wait long.

**Teppanyaki Dining Room** is not exactly
an authentic dose of Japanese cuisine
(Tempura Kiku next door gives a closer
approximation), but it offers a good time.
Guests sit around a large teppan grill and
watch as a nimble chef demonstrates just
how quickly enough chicken, beef, seafood,
and vegetables to feed eight people can be
chopped, seasoned, and stir-fried. Entrées are
sizzling and satisfying. Small parties are
seated together, making the meal a social
affair. Don't wear your finest attire: there's
always the potential for a little splattering
here and there. Reservations are suggested.

## 🍽️ Nine Dragons (China)
**L D** **$$$** ❤️

This stop on Epcot's varied international restaurant tour offers family-style meals prepared in provincial Chinese cooking styles. Entrées include the very spicy Sichaun beef in spicy broth, Xinjiang-style lamb chop, and honey sesame chicken from the Kiangche region of China. The elaborate Beijing duck is carved tableside and served in two courses at dinner time. There's a dim sum bar, too.

Imported Chinese teas, beers, and wines are available. Dessert choices include red-bean ice cream, caramel ginger ice cream, Hainan Sampan, and no-sugar-added chocolate mousse. Reservations are suggested.

## 🏃 Refreshment Port (Canada)
**S** **$** ❤️

A good spot for a quick thirst quencher and a snack on the go. Located on the World Showcase promenade, this is a mini McDonald's. It serves fries, chicken nuggets, frozen desserts, and beverages.

## 🍽️ Rose & Crown Pub and Dining Room (United Kingdom)
**L D S** **$$-$$$** ❤️

Don't let the word "pub" throw you. While this place serves up what is arguably some of the best brews on Walt Disney World property, its dining area is also known for such crowd-pleasing dishes as crispy fish-and-chips, roast prime rib, fresh salmon, and bangers and mash (sausages with mashed potatoes).

For an appetizer, we recommend the sautéed mushrooms in cream sauce with a puff pastry. For dessert there is, among other things, warm apple crumble topped with ice cream and a sticky toffee pudding. Bass ale from England, Tennent's lager and McCaffrey's Cream Ale from Scotland, and Harp lager and Guinness stout, both from Ireland, are on tap. (They're served cold, in the American fashion, not at room temperature, as some Brits prefer.)

The atmosphere is welcoming. It incorporates several architectural styles from the 18th and 19th centuries, which add up to a believable, enjoyable re-creation of the charming pubs so common in the English countryside. In fine weather it's pleasant to lunch under a canopy on the terrace outside and watch the *FriendShip* water taxis cruising across World Showcase Lagoon.

The pub section of the Rose & Crown serves such snacks as Stilton cheese and fresh fruit platters, and fish-and-chips—along with all the brews noted above and traditional British mixed drinks, such as shandies (Bass ale and ginger ale), lager with lime juice, black velvets (Guinness stout and champagne), and black and tans (Bass ale and Guinness stout). This spot is quite popular, so it's often necessary to queue up at the door. But the wait is seldom very long, since few guests choose to linger over their drinks. A piano player is sometimes on hand to entertain revelers. Note that the pub section also spills out onto the promenade—where the first-come, first-served waterside tables make for a nice spot to sip a drink and, possibly, enjoy some fish-and-chips from a nearby stand. Reservations are not available in the pub areas, but are recommended for the adjacent restaurant.

# San Angel Inn (Mexico)

**L D** **$$$**

The lights are low, the mood is romantic, and there is a smoking volcano poised tableside. If that's not enchantment enough, there's a mystical pyramid and a moonlit river. It all takes place inside the pyramid that serves as the Mexico pavilion. (To get there, you'll have to meander through the bustling marketplace known as La Plaza de los Amigos.)

The menu? You might need to bring the table candle closer to read it, but you'll find Mexican fare from margaritas to chicken molé. And there's more: the menu also offers a variety of more subtly flavored fish, poultry, and meat dishes. To start, there's *queso fundido* for two (melted cheese and Mexican pork sausage with corn or flour tortillas).

As entrées, the menu offers grilled tenderloin of beef served with a chicken enchilada, guacamole, and refried beans; *plato Mexicano* (beef taco, quesadilla, and refried beans for lunch; at dinner substitute beef tenderloin or *tampiquena* for the quesadilla); and *ensalada Mexicana* (mixed greens with grilled chicken, tomatoes, avocado, turnip, cheese, and cactus strips tossed in a tortilla shell). Mexican desserts are largely unfamiliar to North Americans, with the possible exception of the custard known as flan, but are well worth trying. Dos Equis beer and margaritas make good accompaniments. Reservations are suggested. Note that some dishes may have a little kick. Ask your server if you're concerned. They can steer you toward less spicy selections. Of course, if you crave more heat, there's a nice supply of hot sauce at the ready.

### 🏃 Sommerfest (Germany)
**L D S** **$-$$** ✿

Here, quick sustenance takes such classic
forms as bratwurst, soft pretzels (if they're too
dry, we send them back), ham sandwiches,
Black Forest cake, and apple strudel. The
nicely shaded outdoor seating area sports a
festive mural. Löwenbräu beer is offered at
this outdoor establishment, located toward
the rear of the pavilion.

### 🏃 Tangerine Cafe (Morocco)
**L D S** **$-$$** ✿

Named for the Moroccan city of Tangier,
this casual spot serves Mediterranean specialties, lentil salad, hummus, and tabbouleh,
as well as rotisserie chicken and lamb presented as sandwiches (served on Moroccan
bread) and combination platters. Specialty
coffees and pastries are available.

## Hot Tip

*If you plan to see IllumiNations, know that
the show takes place nightly, at 9 P.M. Try
to time it so your evening meal winds up
no later than 8:45 P.M.—and tell your
server when you arrive.*

### 🏃 Yakitori House (Japan)
**D S** **$** ✿

Easy to miss, what with its out-of-the-way
location, this is an ideal spot to go to escape
the masses and savor a simple, relaxing meal.
To get there, you'll need to find the path on

the left of the Japan pavilion. The path
deposits you in a peaceful Japanese garden.
The no-frills restaurant sits to the right of
the garden. The fare here includes *guydon*, a
stewlike concoction flavored with soy sauce;
sushi; *edamame* (soybeans); sushi rolls;
teriyaki chicken; Japanese sweets (desserts
include chestnut cake); and beverages.
Drinks include green tea, Kirin beer, and
sake (rice wine served hot or cold).

## CHECK, PLEASE!

Paying for a meal at Disney World is a
piece of cake—especially if you have a
Disney resort ID (and back it up with a
major credit card upon check-in).
Resort IDs are accepted by most
restaurants on WDW property. Notable
exceptions: eateries at the Swan and
Dolphin resorts, some Downtown
Disney spots, Hotel Plaza Blvd. resorts,
and some snack carts. Simply hand it to
the waiter or cashier, sign the bill (don't
forget to add a tip when appropriate),
and the charge will appear on your
hotel statement at checkout.

Of course, there are other ways to
pay the piper. In addition to U.S. currency, which is welcome everywhere,
traveler's checks and major credit
cards are accepted in most non-cart
locations. Foreign currency is a no-no.
Disney currency (aka Disney Dollars)
works like cash in all Disney-owned-
and-operated venues. The Disney Gift
Card is accepted at most WDW
owned-and-operated establishments.

# Disney-MGM Studios

Lights, camera, lunch! This theme park, designed to resemble a working Hollywood backlot circa the 1940s, tackles the role of feeding guests with style and whimsy. Here you can sit in a classic car and enjoy a meal at a drive-in, rub elbows with the beautiful people at a reproduction of the Hollywood Brown Derby, and play the part of sitcom kid as you're served by "Mom" or "Dad" at the 50's Prime-Time Cafe (no elbows on the table, please!). While the attention to theming is obvious, it doesn't upstage the fare. So grab a napkin, and get ready for your close-up.

##  ABC Commissary

**L D S** **$-$$** ♥

Located near the Chinese Theater, this spot
has shaken up the menu a few times of late.
Most recently, it featured fish-and-chips,
vegetable noodle stir-fry, cheeseburgers,
tabbouleh wraps, and Cuban sandwiches.
Dessert items include macadamia turtle tart,
strawberry parfait, and chocolate mousse.
Soft drinks and beer are served. The restaurant itself is huge, and does indeed resemble
an actual studio commissary. We could do
without the ads for ABC shows, which play
on a continuous loop from TVs scattered
throughout the dining area.

## Backlot Express

**L D S** **$-$$** ♥

Designed to look like a crafts shop on an old
studio backlot, this eatery is near the Star
Tours attraction. The indoor seating areas
carry out the prop-shop theme, with paint-
speckled floors, car engines, and various
other spare prop parts. The outdoor tables are
situated amid plants and trees. Menu offerings include burgers, chicken strips, hot dogs,
grilled turkey and cheese sandwiches, grilled
veggie sandwiches, and salads. For dessert,
there's chocolate double-bundt cake, chocolate marshmallow mousse, and strawberry
parfait. Soft drinks and beer are available.

## The Dip Site

**L D S** **$**

A tiny tin shack, which sits beside the
Indiana Jones Epic Stunt Spectacular, the
Dip Site dispenses chips, lemonade, water,
and beer.

# FANTASMIC! DINNER PACKAGE

Guests who make dining arrangements at their Disney resort or at any of the parks can take advantage of the Fantasmic! Dining Opportunity Special. Reserved seating for the evening's performance of Fantasmic! comes with the meal at no extra cost.

Why book the package? Besides guaranteeing a seat for dinner, it ensures that you will get seating for Fantasmic! without having to wait in line. This is critical—since guests start lining up for the show as much as two hours ahead. With the package, you can have a relaxing dinner and head over to the show shortly before it starts.

Call 407-939-3463 for more information or to book a "dinner and a show" package. At press time, the Hollywood Brown Derby, Hollywood and Vine, and Mama Melrose's Ristorante Italiano were participating in the program. (Even though the Fantasmic! Dining Opportunity *may* be available for walk-ups, we highly recommend booking it in advance—you've got nothing to lose.)

## 🍽 50's Prime Time Cafe
**L D** **$$-$$$**

This retreat to the era of *I Love Lucy* is an amusing amalgam of comfort food, kitschy 1950s-style kitchen nooks, and attentive servers of the "No talking with your mouth full" ilk. Nostalgia abounds, with more cookie jars than you could shake an Oreo cookie at, all meant to bring you back to childhood of yesteryear; even the dessert "menu" is read on an old ViewMaster, and TVs broadcast black-and-white clips from favorite fifties comedies (all related to food). Guests are waited on by "Mom" (and other family members) with considerable enthusiasm— they make recommendations and encourage everyone to keep their elbows off the table, eat their vegetables, and clean their plates (or no dessert!).

Adding to the appeal is the menu, which is packed with comfort foods. For openers there's a choice of "homemade" chicken noodle soup or onion rings. Specialties of the house include magnificent meat loaf, served with mashed potatoes and vegetables; fried chicken; and old-fashioned pot roast. There are Caesar salads, sandwiches, and chicken potpie, too. Milk shakes, ice cream sodas, and root beer floats are filling accompaniments. And when you've finished everything on your plate, "Mom" will ask if you'd like dessert. Standouts include s'mores, a graham cracker topped with chocolate and toasted marshmallows (you'll feel like you're back at summer camp); sundaes; seasonal cobbler; and angel food cake with fresh berries and whipped cream. A full bar is available. Kids of all ages love this place. Reservations are suggested.

## BABY NEEDS

Babies. They're a needy lot. Fortunately, most of the requisite supplies can be found somewhere at Disney World—if you know where to look. Formula and jarred food can be purchased at the Baby Care Center in each of the theme parks and at every WDW resort. Most restaurants have kids' menus with toddler-friendly food (mac and cheese, chicken nuggets, and the like).

If your baby is partial to a specific formula or brand of food, consider shipping a box of it to your hotel before you leave home. Keep in mind that there are several grocery stores near Disney World. If you'll have a car, it may be worth the trip (a guest relations clerk can offer directions). The selections are more varied, as are the prices. Stash perishables in an in-room refrigerator—they rent for about $10 per night in WDW "value" resorts and are free in the "deluxe" and "moderate" resorts. It's best to request one when you make your reservation. Some other points of interest regarding baby diners at WDW:

• Most eateries have high chairs and booster seats. Request one when you make your restaurant reservation.
• Stroller use inside restaurants is discouraged. Park it outside.

**Continued on page 54**

**Continued from page 53**

• WDW restaurants are often chilly. Be sure to pack a sweater or blanket.

• Be it a fast-food or table-service restaurant, bring toys to keep the little one busy.

• The following resorts have 24-hour snack bars: Grand Floridian, Polynesian, Contemporary, Dolphin, and Buena Vista Palace (on Hotel Plaza Boulevard). The middle-of-the-night pickin's are slim, but milk and cereal are served 'round the clock.

• If you'd like a quiet spot to nurse an infant, head to a Baby Care Center in any of the theme parks. They all have rooms with rocking chairs.

• If you're headed for a long day in a theme park, pack simple, healthy snacks for toddlers.

• To make your dining experience less harried, consider feeding your baby before you get to the restaurant.

## Hollywood & Vine
**B L D** **$$$** ❤

The exterior is Art Deco and the interior conjures up memories of a 1950s American diner—forged out of stainless steel with pink accents. It's next door to the 50's Prime Time Cafe, just off Hollywood Boulevard.

The buffet breakfast and lunch, known as Playhouse Disney's Play 'N Dine, are character affairs featuring Jo Jo and Goliath from *Jo Jo's Circus* and Leo from *The Little Einsteins*. The morning meal includes

## Hot Tip

*If you can stand to miss the evening's performance of Fantasmic! (the Disney-MGM Studios nighttime spectacular), consider dining in one of the park's popular eateries during the show.*

Mickey waffles, frittatas, fresh fruits, and house-made pastries. Lunch may offer items such as herb-crusted baked salmon with citrus butter, multigrain pasta with plum tomotoes and mushrooms, and salads. Dinner, which is character-free, also features carved meats, peel-and-eat shrimp, and mussels. Some soft drinks are included. Beer and wine are served at an extra cost. Reservations are suggested.

### Hollywood Brown Derby
**LD** **$$–$$$** 🍴

The Studios' most gracious dining is found at this faithful revival of the original *cause célèbre*, which opened on Hollywood and Vine in 1926. Dressed to the nines in chandeliers and celebrity caricatures, the restaurant stokes the appetite with its ever-so-finely chopped signature Cobb salad (invented by Brown Derby owner Bob Cobb) and grapefruit cake—a Brown Derby institution. Some of the fare is a bit highbrow (and high-priced) for the theme park crowd, but if you're up for a splurge, this spot is sure to rise to the occasion. We recommend the fresh sesame-seared ahi tuna; steaks get good marks, too.

The slightly formal atmosphere is not likely to enchant most kids, but simple, youngster-friendly fare is available. The international wine list is excellent. Reservations are suggested.

## Mama Melrose's Ristorante Italiano
**L D** **$$-$$$** ❤

This pleasant Italian restaurant (with a California twist) is located in a large warehouse that has been converted into a dining room. Appetizer flatbreads are prepared in a wood-burning oven. The menu also features risotto, chicken, pasta, and vegetarian options. Dishes include spaghetti with clams, mussels, and calamari in a spicy marinara sauce; osso buco; and spicy Italian sausage. If you like fish, you may enjoy the tuna or salmon; both rate high with us. The wine list includes selections from California and Italy. Reservations are suggested.

## Min and Bill's Dockside Diner
**S** **$**

Mmm . . . milk shakes. 'Nuf said. In addition to some of the greatest, thickest shakes in the World, Min and Bill's waterside snack spot also serves cookies, stuffed pretzels, coffee, soft drinks, and beer. To find it, look for the boat with the line to board, er, buy.

FYI: *Min and Bill* was a 1930s feature film (one of the first talkies) that took place on a waterfront. Hence, the lakefront locale.

## Sci-Fi Dine-In Theater
**L D** **$$-$$$** ❤

A convincing re-creation of a drive-in theater, the atmosphere here is completely absorbing. The tables are actually flashy, 1950s-era cars, complete with fins and whitewalls. Stars twinkle overhead in the "night sky," and drive-in theater speakers are mounted beside each car. All seats are

## Hot Tip

*While the Sci-Fi Dine-In Theater has tables that can accommodate guests who use wheelchairs, there aren't many. Be sure to request such a table when you make your reservations—and confirm it by phone before you go; 407-WDW-DINE (939-3463).*

within cars, with most featuring front- and backseat counters facing front. Not terribly conducive to meaningful table talk, but ideal for viewing the large movie screen, where a 45-minute compilation of the best (and worst) of science-fiction trailers and cartoons plays in a continuous loop. There are a couple of traditional tables within oversize cars—if this is your preference, make that known when you book the table and expect to wait a bit when you arrive.

The eatery is also notable for its huge hot and cold sandwiches. Selections include Reuben sandwiches, chicken sandwiches, barbecue ribs, and shrimp penne pasta. Kids love the mini-burger plate. There's also a slate of desserts, including cheesecake, milk shakes, and hot fudge sundaes. It's a bit on the expensive side, but the "show" aspect is worth it to many. It's popular with guests of all ages. Reservations are suggested.

###  Starring Rolls Cafe

**B L S** **$–$$** ♥

In a hurry? Here's where you can get the day off to a quick start, or take a cookie or a coffee break. Rolls, pastries, muffins, croissants, and sugar-free desserts are sold at this sweet-smelling shop. Coffee (beans are roasted on the premises), tea, and soft drinks are also served. For lunch, sandwiches and wine are available.

### 🏃 Studio's Catering Co. & Flatbread Grill

**S** **$–$$** 🐭

Next to the Honey, I Shrunk the Kids Movie Set Adventure, this spot offers Mediterranean-inspired fare. Among the choices are grilled wraps, Greek salad, chicken stew, and baked goods. There is a full bar serving specialty libations, too. Note that at press time there were rumors of possible menu changes.

### 🏃 Sunset Ranch Market

**L D S** **$–$$**

A celebration of California's outdoor lifestyle, this open-air cluster of snack stands has something for everyone. **Rosie's All-American Cafe (🐭)** sells cheeseburgers, chicken strips, and soups. **Catalina Eddie's (🐭)** offers plain and pepperoni pizzas, plus side salads, chocolate cake, and apple pie. Fruit, juice, and soft drinks are available at **Anaheim Produce. Toluka Legs Turkey Co. (🐭)** serves turkey legs and chili dogs. For breakfast, it may have bagels, Danish, muffins, and cereal. **Hollywood Scoops Ice Cream** offers creamy treats (including sugar-free vanilla). **Fairfax Fries** serves McDonald's fries and soft drinks.

### 🏃 Toy Story Pizza Planet

**L D S** **$–$$** 🐭

Located inside a kid-magnet arcade is this counter-service spot with a limited but youngster-friendly menu. Select from simple individual pizzas, salads, desserts, and juice.

# Disney's Animal Kingdom

**W**alt Disney World's nature-oriented theme park is ideal for grazers: with more than a dozen spots to nosh, it may not be strong on table service, but it takes "quick service" quite seriously. When your stomach starts growling like the beasts at the Kilimanjaro Safaris attraction, consider the top-notch Tusker House and Flame Tree Barbecue. Not only do they offer mouthwatering meals, but they serve them in some of the fanciest fast-food dining environments around.

### 🏃 Anandapur Ice Cream

`S` `$`

This ice-cream truck doesn't actually move, but the Asia-based vehicle does deliver chilly treats. Ice cream is available by the cone, or in a soda float.

### 🏃 Dino Bites

`S` `$` 🟣

In DinoLand U.S.A., on the far side of Chester and Hester's DinoRama, is a small stand that offers desserts throughout the day.

## WATER PARK DINING

Disney's duo of water parks, Typhoon Lagoon and Blizzard Beach, provides plenty of opportunities to defy Mom's plea to wait an hour to splash after you nosh. The fare is limited to the quick-service kind (who wants a sit-down meal in a soggy swimsuit?) and what it lacks in creativity, it makes up for in convenience and appeal: burgers, hot dogs, pizzas, salads, ice cream, and snacks are sold at spots with names like Tilly's Snack Shack (🟣), Leaning Palms (🟣), and Avalunch (🟣). Frozen drink specialties flow at Let's Go Slurpin' (Typhoon Lagoon) and at Blizzard Beach's Polar Pub.

Some folks take the day at the beach theme seriously enough to pack a picnic lunch. Coolers may be brought into both parks, but alcoholic beverages and glass containers may not.

# Hot Tip

*By late summer of 2007, there'll be a new place to rustle up grub in Animal Kingdom. Set in the Anandapur area of the park, the eatery features an Asian-fusion concept and offers table- and quick-service dining.*

### Flame Tree Barbecue

**L D S** | **$–$$** | ❤

If you can't find this eatery, just follow your nose. Because when the kitchen is cooking, the scent is compelling. (It's been known to operate seasonally, so it may not be open during your visit.) It serves up a selection of barbecued sandwiches and platters, all wood roasted. Sample the mild, tomato-based barbecue sauce or the spicy, mustard-based Carolina-style sauce with your smoked beef brisket, pulled pork, and hickory-smoked St. Louis ribs. (Disney's ovens produce 1,200 pounds at a time. Want the recipe? Just ask.) Smoked turkey sandwiches, salads, and key lime pie round out the options.

There's outdoor seating along the river (lovely when it's not 98 degrees). If Flame Tree isn't serving, the tables are still open for use. It's located on Discovery Island, near DinoLand.

### Harambe Fruit Market

**S** | **$**

Sometimes, a crunchy apple is just what the doctor—or the hungry theme park guest—ordered. Apples, among other healthy snacks, are available at this fruit stand near the entrance to Kilimanjaro Safaris.

ANIMAL KINGDOM

###  Kusafiri Coffee Shop & Bakery

`S` `$`

The bakery inside Tusker House provides a steady stream of breakfast treats and assorted desserts, plus cappuccino and espresso.

### Pizzafari

`L D S` `$-$$` ❤

This big, colorful dining area has no-nonsense fare that tends to please young palates. Pizzas are prepared on the specially designed Pizzamatic, which can serve up to 1,200 pizzas per hour (think quantity over quality). Hot Italian-style sandwiches and salad are also on the menu. Animal murals decorate the walls of this restaurant, located on Discovery Island, near the bridge to Camp Minnie-Mickey.

### Rainforest Cafe

`B L D S` `$$-$$$`

Animal Kingdom's original table service restaurant is located at its front entrance. The atmosphere blends well with the theme park it borders. Environmentally conscious cuisine includes items like Planet Earth Pasta and the Plant Sandwich. (The Calypso Dip—fresh salmon, artichoke hearts, onions, spices, and cheese served with warm pita—is consistently yummy.) There's no net-caught fish on the menu, or beef from countries that destroy rain forest land to raise cattle. Fish tanks, tropical decor, and the occasional thunderstorm add to the ambience (and noise level). Kids thrive here.

The restaurant and bar are accessible from inside and outside Animal Kingdom, so admission to the park isn't necessary to

ANIMAL KINGDOM

enter. (There is another location at Downtown Disney Marketplace.) Reservations are suggested for all meals.

##  Restaurantosaurus
**B L D S** **$–$$** ☺

Hang a right once you enter DinoLand U.S.A., and you'll discover this spot. Themed as a campsite for student paleontologists, this eatery is filled with fossils, bones, and such; class notes line the walls. The kitchen offers fast food at lunch and dinner: burgers, chicken salad, and hot dogs—plus McDonald's fries, chicken nuggets, and Happy Meals. Breakfast is a popular, all-you-can-eat, character-hosted buffet called Donald's Prehistoric Breakfastosaurus. The experience is generally entertaining, powered by the antics of resident students, who wait tables between classes. Cost is $18.99 for adults; $10.99 for kids ages 3 through 9. Reservations are suggested for the breakfast buffet. Book early. (As fast-food affairs, lunch and dinner require no advance reservations.)

##  Tamu Tamu Refreshments
**S** **$**

This walk-up window dispenses soft-serve frozen yogurt and ice-cream cones, floats, and sundaes. There's a small seating nook next door. It's in Harambe, just across the way from Tusker House.

##  Tusker House
**L D S** **$–$$**

As fast food goes, the Tusker House fare is head, shoulders, and antlers above the rest.

We dig the carved chairs inside, but somehow the Safari Amber beer tastes better outside under the thatched roof. The menu—which is one of the best in Animal Kingdom—features rotisserie chicken cooked in a 16-foot "wall of flames." Other highlights may include grilled salmon, chicken salad, vegetable sandwiches served with fruit, fried chicken sandwiches, and

## Hot Tip

*Restaurantosaurus and Rainforest Cafe may be the only Animal Kingdom eateries to serve a full breakfast for most of 2007, but a few spots, including Coffee Kiosk (a stand near the Tip Board in front of the Tree of Life) and Kusafiri Coffee Shop and Bakery, offer breakfast items. That said, don't arrive starving, as you may have to do a bit of foraging.*

turkey wraps with corn chowder. Side dishes such as fresh vegetables and mashed potatoes round out the creative options. It's on the left side of Harambe, just over the bridge from Discovery Island. Note that the Kusafiri Coffee Shop & Bakery is inside. For details, see page 62.

## Hot Tip

*That gift card burning a hole in your pocket? Know that the WDW Shopping & Dining Gift Card may be redeemed at all Disney-owned-and-operated dining, shopping, and recreation locations where credit cards are accepted.*

# Downtown Disney

This enclave of shopping, dining, and entertainment has three distinct neighborhoods: the Marketplace, Pleasure Island, and the West Side. Within them, you'll find eateries such as Wolfgang Puck Café, House of Blues, Ghirardelli Soda Fountain and Chocolate Shop, Planet Hollywood, and Rainforest Cafe. Overall, Downtown Disney provides a variety of fast food, table service, cheap eats, and super splurges. Downtown Disney is on Walt Disney World property and can be reached by car or resort bus. Admission is no longer required to enter Pleasure Island, though there is a fee to enter most of the clubs themselves. The other branches of Downtown Disney's entertaining triumvirate are also gate-free, but individual venues may charge a cover.

## 🍽 Bongos Cuban Cafe
## (West Side)
### L D S  $$-$$$

Spicing up the Downtown Disney dining repertoire with a menu driven by Cuban and Latin American flavors, this eatery was created, in part, by singer Gloria Estefan. Its slate of traditional and nouvelle Cuban dishes includes black bean soup (our preferred dish), plantains, steak topped with onions, and flan. The atmosphere here is quite lovely (and often lively). Indoors, the mosaic mural and palm-leaf railings set the scene; the patio for outdoor seating wraps around a three-story pineapple, easily our favorite part of this creatively designed restaurant. A take-out window provides snacks on the go. Diners are sometimes treated to live music (feel free to sway in your seat). Reservations are available by calling 407-828-0999.

## 🍽 Cap'n Jack's Restaurant
## (Marketplace)
### L D S  $$-$$$  🐭

The Cap'n is a true Walt Disney World legend, having the distinction of 30-plus years of seafaring service under his cap. Its fare, like its look, remains timeless. The nautically themed pier house juts right out over Lake Buena Vista, providing water views from most vantage points. The appetizer menu is such—crab cakes, clam chowder, and the like—that it's as good for lunch or dinner as it is for a snack. Entrées extend to salmon, lobster, mahimahi, seafood pasta, and "landlubber" specials (i.e. steak). There is a tempting variety of wines, beer, and other cocktails—and the house's signature frozen strawberry margaritas are classic.

Cap'n Jack's is a nice place to enjoy the late afternoon, as the setting sun streams through the picture windows. Tables are available on a first-come, first-served basis.

## 🏃 Cheesecake Factory Express (West Side)

**L D S** **$-$$**

If your time at DisneyQuest (a multistory arcade at Downtown Disney West Side) straddles a meal hour, you may consider dining at the Cheesecake Factory Express. (It is the only option in the building.)

The daily offerings are prepared fresh from the three main counters. Highlights include warm spinach and artichoke dip served with chips and salsa, pizza, and pannini sandwiches (grilled chicken, chicken and mushroom, and Italian). Also available are a selection of salads and several specialty burgers and hot dogs. Desserts come in the form of frozen mud pie, hot fudge brownie sundaes, cookies, cakes, and, of course, cheesecake. *Note that DisneyQuest admission is required to eat here.*

## 🏃 Earl of Sandwich (Marketplace)

**B L D S** **$-$$** 🐭

This establishment is brimming with sweet and savory possibilities. Among the fare standing by for snackers is a variety of hot and cold sandwiches (freshly prepared on warm bread), tossed salads, and homemade desserts. There are ice-cream sandwiches, too. Breakfast items include sandwiches and baked goods. There are quite a few "grab and go" selections, too. Seating is available in the shop and along the waterfront on Lake Buena Vista.

## ☛ Fulton's Crab House (Marketplace)

**L D S** **$$$–$$$$**

This regal restaurant, once known as the *Empress Lilly* (after Walt Disney's wife Lillian Disney), occupies a three-deck river-boat. Though it looks as though it might set sail at any moment, the replica ship is permanently docked at the edge of Lake Buena Vista. Guests board the ship via gangplank and are enveloped by polished woods, brass detailing, and nautical nostalgia.

The extensive (albeit pricey) dinner menu changes with the day's arrivals. It's not unusual for Hawaiian albacore tuna (accompanied by, say, crab bordelaise and corn-whipped potatoes) to be seen next to Great Lakes walleyed pike (with garlic chips and herbed rice). Standbys include Dungeness crab cakes; cioppino, a San Francisco–style stew with seafood galore in a tomato broth; garlic chicken; crab and lobster platters; and filet mignon.

For a quicker fix, visit our top choice here: the ravishing raw bar at the adjoining Stone Crab lounge. In fact, for a relatively reasonably priced lunch, it's lounge or bust. If the weather's pleasant, try for a table outside, on the bow of the ship. Reservations are suggested for the restaurant.

DOWNTOWN DISNEY

## 🏃 Ghirardelli Soda Fountain and Chocolate Shop (Marketplace)

**S** **$–$$**

What is it about an old-fashioned ice cream parlor that makes just about everybody giddy? Oh, yes, the ice cream. This spot

*Do you have a WDW Annual Pass? If so, know that many Disney World eateries offer lunchtime discounts for you and up to three guests. Lunch hours vary from place to place, and alcohol is not included. Inquire when you make your reservations.*

does it one better and throws in its famous chocolate, to boot. Stop in for a chocolaty treat, root beer float, or refreshing malt. If you've got a sweet tooth, this place delivers. Tables are available on a first-come, first-served basis. You may even get a free sample.

### House of Blues (West Side)
**L D S** **$$–$$$**

With a distinctive southern-inspired menu (étouffée, jambalaya, barbecue, catfish nuggets, and the like) and rustic, folk art–studded design, this Disney-based member of the House of Blues family of restaurants doesn't disappoint. At the far west of the West Side, it's a satisfying spot for an afternoon meal, dinner, or a late-night bite. The enclosed Voodoo Garden is particularly inviting. Live music is presented in the restaurant and on the front porch on select days. There is a lively gospel brunch every Sunday. Reservations are recommended. To book a table, call 407-934-BLUE.

### McDonald's (Marketplace)
**B L D S** **$**

No surprises here. Okay, the salad selection may come as a surprise (there are three to choose from), but other than that, this is a classic Mickey D's experience. This branch of the Golden Arches is located on the western edge of the Marketplace.

## 🍽 Planet Hollywood (West Side)
**L D S** **$$-$$$** 🍷

Chances are, you'll have no trouble finding this restaurant—just keep your eyes peeled for the giant globe. Built on three levels, this colossal sphere is jam-packed with classic movie and television memorabilia.

The menu features salads, sandwiches, pasta dishes, above-average burgers, appetizers, fajitas, and dessert specialties. Consider sampling the chicken crunch appetizer, Asian chicken salad, shrimp and bacon club sandwich, or lasagna. Bananas Foster is among the dessert choices. Reservations are not available.

## 🍽 Portobello Yacht Club (Marketplace)
**D** **$$$**

Portobello's design combines high gables and beamed ceilings, bright Mediterranean colors, and earthy tones.

The open kitchen turns out grilled meat and fish and small pizzas baked in a wood-burning oven. Try the *quattro formaggi,* a four-cheese pie that's a great appetizer or snack. Pasta offerings include *spaghettini alla Portobello* (pasta with shrimp, scallops, clams, mussels, crab legs, tomatoes, garlic, olive oil, wine, and herbs) and *penne all' amatriciana* (long pasta tubes with plum tomatoes, mushrooms, pancetta, garlic, onions, and fresh herbs). There's a nice wine list, too. Be sure to save room for desserts such as *crema brucciata,* white-chocolate custard with a caramelized sugar glaze; or *paradiso al cioccolato,* a layer cake with chocolate ganache frosting, chocolate toffee crunch filling, and warm caramel sauce. Portobello also offers specialty coffees, while the wine list consistently receives the *Wine Spectator* award. Reservations are suggested.

## 🍽️ Raglan Road (Pleasure Island)

`S` `$$-$$$` 🐭

A wee bit of the Emerald Isle has joined the scene at Disney's Pleasure Isle. The cozy spot—which replaced the Pleasure Island Jazz Company in 2005—features furnishings crafted in Ireland, live music, and a menu with cuisine courtesy of Chef Kevin Dundon, one of Ireland's best-known culinary wizards. Think traditional Irish fare with a modern flair. There is no admission charge to enter—be it for food and/or drink.

## 🍽️ Rainforest Cafe (Marketplace)

`L D S` `$$-$$$`

Lush (and loud) as a jungle, this place is thick with tropical vegetation and fish-filled aquariums (not to mention the occasional thunderstorm). A talking tree offers a stream of ecological insights, and animal experts are on hand to field questions. Dishes have names like Mogambo (pasta with shrimp), Plant Sandwich (veggies), and Mojo Bones (barbecued ribs). Appetizers and desserts can be shared. Reservations can be made by calling the restaurant: 407-827-8500. Without it, expect a wait. Note that there is another Rainforest Cafe at Disney's Animal Kingdom. (The Animal Kingdom location accepts reservations through 407-WDW-DINE [939-3463].)

### ⚡ Wetzel's Pretzels
### (West Side and Marketplace)

**S** $

Salted or unsalted, buttery or plain—Wetzel's can satisfy most pretzel cravings. Among the choices are the Jalapeño Cheese Melt, the Sinful Cinnamon, and the Three-Cheese varieties. They sell ice cream, too.

### 🍽 Wolfgang Puck Café
### (West Side)

**L D S** $$$

One of four Walt Disney World establishments that bear the name "Wolfgang Puck," this one offers some of the chef's best-known specialties. Among the spotlighted dishes are gourmet pizzas, Thai chicken satay, pasta with fresh vegetables, Chinois Chicken Salad, and rotisserie chicken. The menu is equal parts sophisticated and straightforward—and very fresh. Plan ahead and save room for dessert—the sweets are merely sensational. The place is a bit noisy, but worth shouting over.

Sushi lovers take note: housed within this space is a sushi bar that's as aesthetically

## SMOKE SCREEN

With the exception of designated outdoor areas, all public parts of the theme parks and resorts are strictly nonsmoking. Tobacco products are no longer sold in the parks. Florida law prohibits smoking inside public areas, such as bars, shops, and restaurants.

appealing as it is palate pleasing. You can order sushi at the bar and in the cafe. Reservations are suggested.

### 🍽 Wolfgang Puck Café— The Dining Room (West Side)
**D** **$$$–$$$$** ✧

Don't be confused by the name. The Dining Room refers to a separate restaurant that just happens to be in the same building as Wolfgang Puck Café and Express. (We think of it as "Puck's Deluxe.") The formal upstairs Dining Room is devoted to the more elaborate of Wolfgang Puck's cuisine—for example, Chinois rack of lamb with a spicy cilantro-mint sauce and wasabi-infused pota-toes. Reservations are suggested.

### 🏃 Wolfgang Puck Express (Marketplace and West Side)
**L D S** **$–$$** ✧

Wolfgang Puck turns his talents to fast service and signature treats, including wood-fired pizzas, rotisserie chicken, soups, sandwiches, and fresh salads—including his famous Chinois Chicken Salad. (The West Side location is inside the Wolfgang Puck Café building, while the Marketplace spot is by Disney Days of Christmas.)

## Hot Tip

*The Official All-Star Cafe, located at Disney's Wide World of Sports Complex, is a table-service participant in the Disney Dining Plan.*

## ATTENTION, COFFEE SNOBS

Face it. For many of us, the magic doesn't start until that first sip of coffee makes its way past our lips. And not just any coffee will do. It must be a half-caf, soy-milk latte with extra foam! In other words, we have great expectations. The bad news? The standard cup here is Nescafé. If you're a fan, you're in luck. If not, you may have to venture a bit to get a satisfying java jolt. The good news is, specialty coffee and espresso bars are easing their way onto the Disney scene. There's at least one in each theme park and some at the resorts. Select restaurants serve special coffee blends, too. Among our favorite spots:

- American Adventure (Epcot's World Showcase, a stand near the pavilion)
- Artist Point (Wilderness Lodge)
- Big River Grille & Brewing Works (BoardWalk resort)
- California Grill (Contemporary resort)
- Contemporary Grounds (Contemporary resort, lobby)
- Flying Fish Cafe (BoardWalk resort)
- 40 Thirst Street (Downtown Disney Marketplace and West Side)
- Fresh—Mediterranean Market (Dolphin resort)
- Kona Cafe (Polynesian resort)
- Picabu (Dolphin resort)
- Starring Rolls Cafe (Disney-MGM Studios)
- Writer's Stop (Disney-MGM Studios)

# WDW RESORTS

**E**ach of the nearly 30 resorts at Walt Disney World offers its own set of specially themed eateries. There are clambakes at the Beach Club, luaus at the Polynesian, wild game at the Wilderness Lodge, and beignets at Port Orleans French Quarter. Meals may be served buffet, family, or traditional table-service or fast-food style. Disney characters are often on hand (especially for breakfast), and some snack spots stay open 'round the clock. In fact, the resort dining scene has expanded and been upgraded so much of late that the (occasionally arduous) task of resort-hopping is a more worthwhile experience than ever before.

# ALL-STAR RESORTS

 **Food Courts**

**B L D S** **$–$$** 🐭

Each of the All-Star resorts features a themed central food court. **All-Star Sports** has **The End Zone** food court in **Stadium Hall.** At **All-Star Music,** it's **Intermission** food court in **Melody Hall.** And at the **All-Star Movies** resort, it is the **World Premiere** food court in **Cinema Hall.** The food courts offer similar food stands— although the Movies is a cut above. (It's a bit bigger, brighter, and more modern.) The selections include pasta, pizza, burgers, hot dogs, sandwiches, salads, snacks, and a wide variety of breakfast and baked goods, plus a selection of "grab and go" items. Expect to find lots of kid-pleasers.

# ANIMAL KINGDOM LODGE

 **Boma—Flavors of Africa**

**B D** **$$–$$$** 🐭

Designed to resemble an African market-place, Boma offers an impressively diverse selection—the fare served represents 50 African countries. Though the eatery may be described as "cafeteria style," this is not a negative. It's one big buffet with multiple stations, and the food is every bit as good as what you would expect to find in a fine dining place.

The all-you-can-eat affair provides a tremendous bang for your dining buck.

Menu selections include rotisserie prime rib, salmon, and chicken, plus soups and stews (pumpkin cheese soup and plantain corn stew among them), and watermelon rind salad; be sure to leave room for decadent Kahlua pastry. It's easy to overeat at a bounteous feast such as this, so consider taking tiny portions of everything. You can go back for seconds (or thirds) of your favorites. The wine list includes selections from various African vineyards. Even if you're not staying at the Lodge, it's worth the trip. Reservations are strongly suggested.

## Jiko—The Cooking Place
**D** **$$$-$$$$** ❤

One of the most unusual Walt Disney World dining experiences, Chef Anette Grecchi Gray's cuisine is inspired by the tastes of Africa, with influences from around the globe. Start with one of the paper-thin flatbreads, like kalamata olive with five cheeses, or the unusual cucumber, tomato, and red-onion salad with a watermelon vinaigrette. Pan-roasted fish is a signature dish, but you'll always find filet mignon and braised lamb shank on the menu, too. End your meal with a fabulous cheese course, and/or sweets such as the Jiko Dream-sicle, or Tanzanian chocolate candies.

The impressive wine list is exclusively South African, one of the most extensive collections in the U.S. The ethereal dining room was designed by Jeffrey Beers, a nod to the opening scenes of *The Lion King*. This is an excellent choice for a grown-up splurge. Though it's hardly a kid favorite (the international, sometimes exotic cuisine may not appeal to timid palates), there are child-friendly menu options. Reservations are strongly suggested. Incidentally, the word *jiko* is Swahili for "the cooking place."

##  The Mara

**B L D S** **$-$$** ♥

This enormous place near the pool has several stations from which to order hot entrée selecions. Guests walk up to the counter and place an order. After receiving their order, guests then pay at the cashier and grab a table. There's a substantial "grab and go" department, too. Among the pre-packaged options are sandwiches, salads, fruit, and bakery items.

# BOARDWALK

## Big River Grille & Brewing Works

**l D S** **$$-$$$** ♥

A standout for its fresh-brewed ales alone, this unassuming place delivers huge portions of pub grub. The straightforward menu runs from the likes of burgers and steaks to yellowfin tuna. Sandwiches are a cut above. This restaurant tends to be more low-key than other BoardWalk eateries, and makes for a peaceful retreat during the day. The interior has an industrial feel. We prefer to sit at outdoor tables on the boardwalk. Seating is available on a first-come, first-served basis.

## BoardWalk Bakery

**B S** **$** ♥

On any given morning, there are lines out the door of this tiny bakeshop next door to

Spoodles. (If you're staying at the BoardWalk resort, this is one of the places to get your morning Nescafé.) The menu of fresh-baked goods includes muffins, doughnuts, croissants, and cookies. They have sandwiches and salads, too. Look through the display windows and watch the bakers at work—actually, you'd have to be up by 5 A.M. to catch the entire show, because that's when this daily dose of Disney magic begins.

## ESPN Club
**L D S** **$$-$$$**

For sports fans, this joint is nothing short of a miracle. The spacious, welcoming, occasionally frenzied bar/family restaurant is a hard-core sports club. If there's a game being played, chances are it's on one of the million (okay, 100—but it feels like a lot more) TVs. If not, a simple request may result in a channel change.

The standard fare includes burgers, wings that are larger and yummier than most (and available by the bucket), sandwiches, and a variety of salads and entrées.

## Flying Fish Cafe
**D** **$$$-$$$$**

Fun, sophisticated decor from the designer of the Contemporary's California Grill elevates the appeal—in fact, this restaurant could give most fine, big-city dining spots a run for their money. (Expect the tab to rival cosmopolitan hot spots, too.)

As an example of the exhibition kitchen's knack for light, creatively prepared dishes, consider barbecue-glazed salmon with sweet-corn pudding and potato-wrapped yellowtail snapper—some favorites include the

Peeky Toe crab cake appetizer, the roasted beet salad, and the steak. The menu items vary daily, but steaks and vegetarian choices are usually offered. Though we've yet to be blown away by the service, the recently tweaked menu is worthy of the hefty price tag. Diners may sit at the counter (when doing so, we prefer to sit as far from the open flames of the grill as possible). Reservations are strongly suggested.

## Seashore Sweets'

**S** $

A cheery, old-fashioned sweetshop, this spot sells homemade candies, saltwater taffy, and ice cream and frozen yogurt. Specialty coffees are also offered. It's next door to Flying Fish Cafe.

## Spoodles

**B D** $$-$$$

A big, open dining room accented with flashes of color and butcher-block tables, this family restaurant boasts a Mediterranean menu. All items are prepared in the display kitchen.

Dinner menus highlight specialties from Greece, Spain, North Africa, and Italy and encourage diners to share dishes and try new foods. Offerings range from pizza to braised lamb shank with a creamy herb polenta. Breakfast is strictly an à la carte affair (a buffet is no longer offered). All the expected breakfast foods are available: eggs, bacon, sausage, cereal, and French toast, plus a few more exotic concoctions. A take-out window allows passersby to pick up pizza by the slice. Reservations are suggested.

# CARIBBEAN BEACH

## 🏃 Old Port Royale Food Court

**B L D S** **$-$$** 🐭

A cluster of side-by-side, walk-up windows, this food court caters to families. **Cinnamon Bay Bakery** serves croissants, freshly baked rolls, pastries, ice cream, and other high-calorie treats. Italian specialties are the order at the **Kingston Pasta Shop**. Soups, salads, and hot and cold sandwiches make up the selections at **Montego's Deli**. Burgers and grilled chicken sandwiches are among the offerings at **Port Royale Hamburger Shop**. And pizza is available by the slice or the pie at **Royale Pizza Shop**. There is a spacious dining area, so it's usually easy to get a table.

## 🍽 Shutters at Old Port Royale

**D S** **$$-$$$** 🐭

Though the pirate theme is gone, this cozy dining room is still as kid-friendly as any table-service restaurant can be. Menu highlights include prime rib, lamb chops, and pork loin. The restaurant is within the resort's Old Port Royale building, across from the food court. In addition to soft drinks, beer, wine, and cocktails are served. Reservations are strongly suggested.

## Hot Tip

*Several windows at the Old Port Royale food court offer special kid's meals. They come in a sand bucket!*

**WDW RESORTS**

# CONTEMPORARY

## California Grill
**D** **$$$–$$$$**

The large number of people who return here year after year attests to this restaurant's dedication to excellence. The fresh, seasonal ingredients credo gets an artistic interpretation at this casual feast for the eyes (as well as the stomach) on the Contemporary resort's 15th floor.

The West Coast theme shines through in such dishes as grilled pork tenderloin with balsamic vinegar–smothered mushrooms and polenta. The wine list is a striking mix of greatest hits and good finds. (At press time, six vintages were available by the glass, but that may change.) Also drawing a crowd: the Grill's divine California-style pizza, outstanding sushi bar, and a host of vegetarian choices. The goat-cheese ravioli appetizer is a favorite.

Fresh desserts along the lines of warm Valrhona chocolate cake provide the finishing touches, as do sweeping views of the Magic Kingdom (from select seats).

The small-but-spectacular sushi bar, set within the restaurant itself, is always crowded and never fails to elicit raves. The din in the dining room may impede quiet conversation. Servers occasionally seem to be spread too thin, but the food is consistently first-rate. It also tends to be rather chilly—bring a sweater. Reservations are strongly suggested and must be booked with a credit card. Changes or cancellations must be made at least 24 hours ahead to avoid the $20 per person fee.

There is a special perk available to California Grill patrons—an outdoor area that affords bird's-eye views of the Magic

**B** *breakfast*   **L** *lunch*   **D** *dinner*   **S** *snacks*

Kingdom. When fireworks are presented, the show's sound track is pumped onto this special perch.

Note that all guests must check in on the hotel's second floor.

## Chef Mickey's
**B D** **$$–$$$** 🐭

Sprawling across the cavernous fourth floor of the Contemporary is one of the biggest kid pleasers on Disney property. Here, Chef Mickey and his friends host a buffet-style feast. Colorful illustrations of Disney characters decorate the room, while the monorail occasionally swooshes by in the background. The changing menu takes advantage of seasonal offerings; a sundae bar provides a sweet finish.

This is a popular eatery with a loyal following—and a great place for (informal) birthdays and other celebrations. (We saw a crew of 19 celebrating Grandma and Grandpa's 50th wedding anniversary and the kids—of all ages—were having a blast.)

At some point during the meal, Chef Mickey will stop by your table, as will several of his friends. Be prepared to drop your fork and swing your napkin with Mickey on a moment's notice. Reservations are strongly suggested (this is one of Walt Disney World's most popular restaurants).

## Snack Bar
**B L D S** **$–$$** 🐭

If you head to the first floor in search of the snack bar that's been there since 1971, you're in for a surprise: it moved! All the way to the fourth floor. As with Disney's other round-the-clock resort snack bars, this spot serves light fare 24/7.

# CORONADO SPRINGS

## Maya Grill

**B D** **$$$** ✿

Guests here dine inside a Mayan pyramid, beside a volcano (dormant, of course). The menu features meat, seafood, and poultry dishes with a Latin American flair—some prepared with traditional Mayan seasonings such as achiote (which is blended with sour orange and onions to provide a delicate flavor and golden color). Other choices have more of a Caribbean influence (sweet fried plaintains, yucca fries, and more) and others hail from the American Southwest (T-bone steaks, pork, and lamb). Many items are cooked over an open-pit, wood-fire grill. Breakfast is an all-you-can-eat buffet. Reservations are suggested.

## Pepper Market

**B L D S** **$-$$** ✿

Modeled after an open-air market, there is a large seating area and lots of food stands to choose from. The place is actually a food court with a twist: upon arrival, guests are escorted to a table by a host or hostess and presented with a napkin and a ticket. After that, it's self-service. Would-be diners step up to stands where vendors sell pizza, sand-wiches, salads, burgers, stir-fry, Mexican spe-cialties, baked goods, margaritas, and more. Items are logged on the aforementioned ticket. Just about anything can be ordered "to go." Everything is paid for at meal's end, as guests file past the cashier at the exit. Note that a 10 percent gratuity is automatically included whether you eat in the dining area or not.

WDW RESORTS

# DISNEY'S OLD KEY WEST

### 🏃 Good's Food to Go
`B L D S` `$` 🐭

A walk-up window with a simple menu: hamburgers, cheeseburgers, grilled chicken sandwiches, salads, ice cream, and breakfast selections are among the offerings. It may be possible to order something from the neighboring Olivia's Cafe menu. Just ask.

### 🍽 Olivia's Cafe
`L D` `$$–$$$` 🐭

We thoroughly enjoy the Key Western manner with which Olivia's approaches its

---

## iN-ROOM REFRiGERATORS

Hotel rooms in "deluxe" and "moderate" WDW resorts come with mini fridges. (If it's not in the room when you arrive, call Housekeeping.) Guests staying at "value" resorts may rent a refrigerator for about $10 a night. Request it when you book the room and confirm at least once before arrival. They take up a bit of room, but the fridges are handy for milk and baby products, snacks, and small amounts of groceries. Guests who must store insulin or other medical supplies will not be charged for refrigerator use (a copy of the prescription may be required).

theme. The laid-back setting and menu convey the spirit of the leisure-centric locale. Menu items include salads, conch chowder, baked mahimahi, conch fritters, and seven-layer fudge cake. Great burgers and sandwiches, too. Wine, beer, and cocktails are served. The menu changes seasonally. Reservations are suggested.

# FORT WILDERNESS

## Trail's End Restaurant
**B L D S** | **$–$$** | ♥

True, it's a bit out of the way for anyone but Fort Wilderness guests (and even for some of them!), but for many, this rustic and unassuming spot is well worth the trip.

The informal log-walled restaurant offers a reasonably priced, all-you-can-eat breakfast (arguably one of the biggest bargains on Disney World property). The fare's not exactly gourmet, but it is bountiful. Buffet selections include grits, biscuits, gravy, and a tasty "breakfast pizza" that vaguely resembles an omelet. Lunch features chicken, pizza, soup, and chili. For dinner, expect smoked pork ribs, peel-and-eat shrimp, fried chicken, carved meats, a salad bar, and a variety of sides and dessert items. Pizza is available every night from 4 P.M. until 10 P.M. (until midnight on weekends). Beer, wine, and soft drinks are served (soft drinks and beer are available by the pitcher). Reservations are suggested. Breakfast is $11.99 for adults, $7.99 for kids; lunch is $12.99 for adults, $8.99 for kids; dinner is $19.99 for adults, $9.99 for kids. After the meal, many guests chat and relax in the rocking chairs on the front porch.

## DINNER AT SEA

For Disney's ultimate dinner-and-a-show splurge, consider reserving the elegant *Grand 1* yacht. You and up to 12 lucky invitees can enjoy a private tour of the lakes near the Magic Kingdom capped off with a viewing of Wishes, the park's fireworks show—all the while devouring delightful delicacies prepared by chefs at the Grand Floridian resort. The possibilities range from an intimate cruise for two, complete with dinner and champagne, to a swinging cocktail party for 13, with a boatload of shrimp, chips, wings, beer, and wine.

It costs about $400 (plus tax) per hour to rent the 5-room floating fantasyland. A driver and deckhand are included; refreshments are not. To book, call 407-824-2682 at least 24 hours and up to 90 days ahead. To cater the affair, call 407-824-2578. The *Grand 1* docks at the Grand Floridian but can pick up passengers at the Contemporary, Polynesian, and Wilderness Lodge.

# GRAND FLORIDIAN

### Cítricos
### D $$$–$$$$ ♥

From the aromas wafting from the open kitchen, it's clear that the chef has vowed to wow you with cuisine from the Americas and southern Europe herb by fragrant herb.

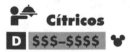
$ *under $14*  $$ *$15-$29*  $$$ *$30-$50*  $$$$ *$51 and up*  **87**

**WDW RESORTS**

The fare varies seasonally, but may include such items as sautéed shrimp with tomato, lemon, and feta cheese; seared tuna with saffron pappardelle; or braised veal shank. Adventurous adult palates are most at home here. The menu's not extensive, but the wine list certainly is. The menu suggests a wine to pair with an appetizer, entrée, and dessert. For $25, the waiter will bring you a glass with each course. There is a private party room for parties of up to 14. Some tables afford views of the Seven Seas Lagoon. Reservations are suggested. Note that Cítricos is closed Monday and Tuesday.

## Gasparilla Grill & Games
**B L D S** **$–$$**

One of the better resort "snack bars," the mainstays at this 24-hour restaurant near the marina are grilled chicken, burgers, pizza, hot dogs, and soft-serve ice cream. Fruit, cereal, packaged snacks, soft drinks, beer, and wine are also available. There is indoor and outdoor seating (beside the resort's marina). Items may be ordered "to go." Continental breakfast is also available. There's a selection of arcade games, too.

## Grand Floridian Cafe
**B L D** **$$$**

A pleasant spot any time of day (there's so much old-world atmosphere here, you'd almost expect to see ladies twirling parasols in the midday sun and Scott Joplin playing "The Entertainer" on a grand piano), it's a relatively reasonably priced, low-key way to check out the poshest WDW resort.

The à la carte breakfast extends a bit beyond the usual fare. The lunch and dinner

## ONE LUMP OR TWO?

Teatime with all the trimmings—scones, tiny sandwiches, and pastries served on bone china—is 2 P.M. in the Garden View lounge at the Grand Floridian. A large selection of teas and tasty accompaniments is offered every day until 6 P.M. Reservations are recommended.

menus vary with the seasons but feature traditional American dishes: onion soup, burgers, and the signature Grand Floridian sandwich. The wine selection is excellent. The restaurant is closed from 11 A.M. to 11:45 A.M. each day. Reservations are suggested, but it's usually possible to get a table if you are willing to wait.

### Narcoossee's
**D** **$$$-$$$$** ❤

Named for a nearby Central Florida town, Narcoossee's specializes in fresh fish dishes —with the occasional land-based entrée making surf-and-turf combinations a decadent possibility. The menu has upscale selections (and prices), but the atmosphere is casual and, more than occasionally, clamorous. The display kitchen presents dishes such as steamed muscles, wild salmon, fresh Maine lobster, and filet mignon. The international wine selection is quite good—you might even enjoy a predinner glass on the veranda. The view of the Seven Seas Lagoon and the Magic Kingdom (in the distance) completes the experience. Reservations are strongly suggested.

## 1900 Park Fare
**B D** **$$$** ☙

The atmosphere is reminiscent of an old-time amusement park, but the sophisticated buffet menu and subtle decor make this one of the most elegant character restaurants on the property. Mary Poppins and friends (characters vary) mingle with guests during the bountiful daily breakfast. Cinderella and her cronies visit the dining room during the dinner hours. Keep in mind that the lineup of characters does change from time to time.

Dinner features hot and cold seafood, pastas, vegetables, breads, and prime rib. The offerings change weekly, and some may be customized. A salad bar and dessert bar stand nearby. There's a special children's buffet, too (though grown-ups have been known to enjoy it). It offers hot dogs, burgers, pizza, chicken nuggets, and a fresh vegetable medly. The restaurant's focal point is Big Bertha, a band organ built in Paris nearly a century ago. She sits in a proscenium and rises 15 feet above the floor, occasionally bursting into a musical serenade, simultaneously playing pipes, drums, bells, cymbals, castanets, and a xylophone. Reservations are strongly suggested.

## Victoria & Albert's
**D** **$$$$**

This elegant dining room has the distinction of being Central Florida's only five-diamond restaurant, an honor awarded by AAA. It is indulgent without being too haute to handle (although the steep prices may curb your enthusiasm) and is considered by many to be the grande dame of the Walt Disney World dining scene.

The seven-course prix fixe menu changes daily, always offering a selection of fish, poultry, beef, veal, or lamb selections, as well as a choice of soups, salads, and desserts. The $100-per-person adventure begins with the arrival of hors d'oeuvres. As an example of what could follow, consider Oriental shrimp dumplings, chicken consomme with pheasant breast, poached Maine lobster with passion fruit butter, mixed field greens with raspberry-pinot noir vinaigrette, and a dark chocolate and strawberry soufflé. Perfect portions keep it all surprisingly manageable. The strains of a harp or violin provide a romantic backdrop. The wine list is encyclopedic. Wine-pairing is available for an additional $55 per person (let your server know about any personal wine preferences).

At the end of the meal, guests are given a souvenir menu and a red rose (ladies only). In sum, though the experience is an extremely expensive one, for many it is also quite special. Jackets are required for men. Reservations are necessary.

# POLYNESIAN

### 🏃 Captain Cook's Snack Company

**B L D S**  **$-$$**  ❤

A snack bar with a bit more atmosphere than usual, Captain Cook's dispenses snacks and light fare 24 hours a day. It's a good spot for breakfast, hamburgers, fruit, salads, cereal, sandwiches, and snacks. Milk (plain and chocolate), beer, wine, and soft drinks are also available. At press time this snack bar was slated for refurbishment and a possible name change.

## Kona Cafe

**B L D S** $$-$$$ 🔴

Warm colors, soft lighting, and a South Seas decor render the crisp, fluid design of this dining space cozy and casual. The menu tends toward the exotic side as far as Disney restaurants are concerned, but there's a nice variety of items to select from. Lunch and dinner menus feature Asian-influenced entrées. Possibilities include teriyaki beef, slow-roasted prime rib, macadamia-crusted mahimahi, and char-crusted strip sirloin in a teriyaki marinade. The morning meal features a more traditional menu. Adjoining the cafe is a coffee counter that's perfect for a quick bite en route to the monorail. Many java junkies claim that the coffee here is the best you'll find on Walt Disney World property. (For other destination coffee spots, refer to page 74.) Reservations are suggested.

## 'Ohana

**B D** $$$ 🔴

'Ohana delivers a classic Disney experience. It's a meticulously themed, family-friendly restaurant, complete with entertainment and a menu that has something for everyone. An interesting twist of note: 'Ohana's family-style dinner experience—a South Pacific feast prepared in the restaurant's prominent open-fire cooking pit—does not come with a menu, so no decisions need to be made. The oak-grilled skewers of turkey, pork, and beef just keep coming. Potatoes au gratin with Maui onions, shrimp, and sesame coriander sticky wings are among the accompaniments, and coconut bread pudding served a la mode with bananas Foster sauce is included for

# HOTEL PLAZA BLVD. RESORTS

The hotels on Hotel Plaza Boulevard—Best Western Lake Buena Vista, Doubletree Guest Suites, Grosvenor, Hilton, Royal Plaza, Buena Vista Palace, and Holiday Inn at Walt Disney World—sit inside WDW boundaries, but are neither owned nor operated by Disney. To make dinner reservations, go to the hotel's front desk. Note that the Holiday Inn was being refurbished at press time and may not reopen in 2007. Here's dining the lowdown:

## Best Western Lake Buena Vista

**Traders Restaurant** serves breakfast and dinner exclusively; the **Parakeet Internet Cafe** offers breakfast, lunch, and dinner, as well as assorted snacks and pizza. The hotel's **Flamingo Cove & Poolside Terrace** serves a full menu for lunch and dinner.

## Doubletree Guest Suites

**Streamers Restaurant** serves up American classics and a breakfast buffet; **Streamers Market** sells snack items and groceries.

## Grosvenor

**Baskervilles Restaurant** incorporates a replica of Sherlock Holmes's office, and serves breakfast and dinner buffets; Disney characters come for breakfast on Tuesday, Thursday, and Saturday; MurderWatch Mystery

*Continued on page 95*

dessert. Soft drinks are included. Beer, wine, and cocktails cost extra.

'Ohana's setting, which features wood carvings under a vast thatched roof, is rather festive. So much so that there are periodic, boisterous, hula hoop, limbo, and coconut-rolling contests for the little ones. Polynesian singers entertain throughout the meal.

Breakfast is also a family affair—make that extended family, as Lilo, Stitch, Mickey, and Pluto host a character meal each morning. Breakfast fare is basic and presented "family style." (Platters are shared by everyone in the party.) Reservations are strongly suggested.

# POP CENTURY

### 🏃 Everything Pop!
**B L D S** | S-$$ | 🐭

The selection at this colorful, modern food court includes pasta, pizza, chicken, burgers, hot dogs, sandwiches, salads, and baked goods (Twinkie tiramasu!).

# PORT ORLEANS FRENCH QUARTER

### 🏃 Sassagoula Floatworks & Food Factory
**B L D S** | S-$$ | 🐭

A food court with a Mardi Gras theme, this spot offers pizza, pasta, gumbo, burgers, sandwiches, soups, salads, spit-roasted

**B** breakfast  **L** lunch  **D** dinner  **S** snacks

Theatre takes place on Saturday at
6 P.M. and 8:45 P.M. **Crumpets Cafe,**
open 24 hours a day, serves continental breakfast and light fare. For
cocktails, there's **Crickets** lounge
and **Moriarty's** pub.

## Buena Vista Palace

The lakeside **Watercress Cafe,**
serves breakfast and lunch only
(Disney characters are in attendance
Sunday morning); the **Watercress
Pastry Shop and Mini Market** is
open from 6 A.M. to midnight, for
baked goods and sandwiches;
**Outback** restaurant (which, despite
the name, is not part of the national
chain) offers seafood and steak; the
**Top of the Palace** lounge provides
the perfect perch to gaze at the sunset
or fireworks over a glass of fine wine.

## Hilton

Cape Cod–themed **Covington Mill**
serves breakfast (with Disney characters
in attendance on Sunday) and lunch
only; **Rum Largo Poolside Cafe**
offers burgers, sandwiches, salads,
and tropical drinks alfresco; **Main-
street Market,** open 24 hours, is
part deli, part country store. For light
meals, snacks, or drinks, drop by
**John T's Lounge** (off the lobby);
after-dinner drinks, coffees, beer, and

**WDW RESORTS**

**Continued on page 96**

**Continued from page 95**

wines by the glass are served at **Mugs Coffee and Wine Bar.**

## Holiday Inn at Walt Disney World

This resort was undergoing a major refurbishment as this book went to press. Details on future eateries were not available at press time, but rest assured that when the hotel finally reopens its guests will not go hungry.

## Hotel Royal Plaza

The **Giraffe Cafe** offers all meals, including an ample breakfast buffet (kids under 10 eat free).

chicken, barbecued ribs, ice cream, and bakery products, including beignets.

# PORT ORLEANS RIVERSIDE

### Boatwright's Dining Hall
**B D** **$$–$$$**

Southern specialties and American comfort food are the big draw here—think prime rib and jambalaya. For breakfast, we favor the banana-stuffed French toast. Beer, wine, and cocktails are available, as are soft drinks. The restaurant is quite popular, and as the resort's only table-service eatery, it's tough to get a table without a reservation. Be sure to book ahead.

###  Riverside Mill
`B L D S` `$-$$` 🐭

This food court disguised as a cotton mill (complete with working waterwheel) boasts half a dozen food counters and a sprawling seating area. Expect to find pizza; pasta; fried, grilled, and roast chicken; burgers; barbecued ribs; salads; sandwiches; fresh baked goods; and other snack selections. There's ample seating, so it's usually possible to get a table even during the busiest of mealtimes.

For guests on the go, the food court's deli does double duty as a convenience store, stocking sandwiches, juice, beer, wine, snack items, and salads.

# SARATOGA SPRINGS RESORT & SPA

###  Artist's Palette
`B L D S` `$-$$` 🐭

Set in a converted artist's loft within Walt Disney World's newest resort, this spot offers breakfast, lunch, and dinner. Among the selections are fresh tossed salads, made-to-order sandwiches, pizza, baked goods, and more. There is an assortment of grocery items to choose from, as well as "grab and go" selections.

### 🍽 The Turf Club
`L D` `$$`

A lounge with an old-fashioned horse-racing theme (and a pool table), this cozy place

**WDW RESORTS**

serves burgers, sandwiches, salmon, snack selections and more. There's a big-screen TV for your sports-viewing pleasure.

# SWAN & DOLPHIN

###  Cabana Bar & Grill

`L S` `$`

Burgers, grilled chicken sandwiches, fruit, and yogurt are offered at this poolside eatery. There is a full bar.

### The Fountain

`L D S` `$$`

Themed as a sophisticated soda fountain, the Dolphin Fountain is a sleek, inviting place to stop for a meal or a sweet snack. Homemade ice cream is the palate-pleasing highlight here. Flavors have included dark chocolate, cappuccino, and mint chocolate chip. Burgers, sandwiches, and salads may also be available.

### Fresh—Mediterranean Market

`B L` `$$–$$$`

A buffet-style eatery, the goal of this sun-drenched Dolphin spot is "to prepare, cook, and serve food in its purest form. . . fresh from the garden or right off the burner." The menu changes seasonally, but you can expect to find salads, sandwiches, and a variety of entrées from the Mediterranean. Made-to-order omelets are offered for breakfast, as is a substantial selection of fresh buffet items. They serve fresh-brewed Starbucks coffee, too.

**WDW RESORTS**

# MEALS WiTH CHARACTER(S)

Character breakfasts are the icing on the cake—or, in some cases, the whole cake—for many visitors to Walt's World. As with everything else here, dining with Donald, munching with Mickey, or chatting with Cinderella is the stuff of everlasting memories. Not surprisingly, these events are extremely popular, so be sure to get reservations (see page 10) to avoid disappointment. One other thing to note: the characters scheduled to appear can change at a moment's notice, and if you are expecting Mickey, you may get Minnie or one of their friends. Here's a rundown of the spots that invite you to dine with Disney characters (characters and other details are subject to change):

### Akershus Royal Banquet Hall:
Belle, Jasmine, Snow White, Sleeping Beauty, and Mary Poppins (see page 34).

### Cape May Cafe:
Goofy, Minnie, Chip, and Dale (see page 107).

### Chef Mickey's:
Mickey, Minnie, Chip, and Dale (see page 83).

### Cinderella's Royal Table:
Cinderella and friends (both breakfast and lunch should be booked well in advance; see page 15). Fairy Godmother is in the house for all meals.

*Continued on page 100*

*Continued from page 99*

**Crystal Palace:**
Winnie the Pooh, Tigger, Eeyore, and
 Piglet (see page 22).
**Garden Grill:**
Chip and Dale (see page 31). Mickey
 and Pluto may join the fun.
**Garden Grove:**
Goofy and Pluto host breakfast at the
 Swan resort (see page 101). Timon and
 Rafiki join them for dinner, when this
 restaurant becomes Gulliver's Grill.
**Hollywood & Vine:**
Enjoy breakfast with Playhouse Disney
 characters Jo Jo, Goliath, and Leo
 (see page 54).
**Liberty Tree Tavern:**
Minnie, Goofy, Pluto, Chip, and Dale
 (see page 20).
**Mickey's Backyard Barbecue:**
Mickey Mouse and friends entertain at
 this Fort Wilderness–based dinner
 show (see page 110).
**1900 Park Fare:**
Stars like Mary Poppins appear at
 breakfast. Cinderella and friends (see
 page 90) are here for dinner. Alice
 and the Mad Hatter host the
 Wonderland Tea Party.
**'Ohana:**
Mickey, Lilo, Stitch, and Pluto (see page
 92).
**Restaurantosaurus:**
Donald, Pluto, and Goofy (see
 page 63).

###  Garden Grove Cafe
**B L D S** $$–$$$

By day, this welcoming greenhouse in the Swan is known as the Garden Grove Cafe. As such, it offers a full breakfast menu and fresh fish, shellfish, and more at lunch. Come dinnertime, the restaurant is transformed into Gulliver's Grill, where large servings are presented before you, and a magician is sometimes on hand to entertain. Desserts are baked fresh daily in an open pastry kitchen. As you approach the restaurant, take a look through the glass windows to see the chefs at work. Character breakfasts are offered on Saturday and Sunday, character dinners take place nightly. Inquire at the restaurant for dates and times, or visit *www.swandolphin.com* for details. Reservations are suggested for dinner.

###  Palio
**D** $$$–$$$$

This sleek Italian trattoria, located at the Swan, is a trusty source of imaginatively prepared homemade pasta, pizza baked in wood-fired ovens, and traditional veal and seafood dishes. (It's also one of the rare WDW spots where you'll see candles on the tables.) Beer and Italian wines are served. Strolling musicians add to the ambience, too. Reservations are suggested.

###  Shula's Steak House
**D** $$$–$$$$

Like the original Shula's in Miami, this Dolphin dining spot specializes in generous portions of certified Angus beef, in addition to chicken and fresh fish dishes. The

**WDW RESORTS**

upscale eatery pays tribute to the 1972 Miami Dolphins—the year legendary coach Don Shula led his team to a perfect NFL season. Photos and souvenirs abound, and the menu comes on an autographed football (yours to keep for about $350). The prices are a bit steep, but the steaks are a cut above. Though the interior celebrates the game of football, this is not a casual sports bar. There isn't a strict dress code, but most guests come in business casual or business, period. (A lot of meals are charged to expense accounts in these parts.) Reservations are recommended for dinner. There is no children's menu.

## Splash Grill

**L S** **$**

A poolside snack bar, this stand serves hamburgers and other grilled fare, as well as ice cream and frozen yogurt. Soft drinks, beer, wine, and frozen specialty cocktails are available, too. An assortment of pack-aged snacks is also on hand.

## Todd English's bluezoo

**D** **$$$–$$$$**

A sophisticated addition to the Disney dining scene, this Dolphin eatery always tempts us with potential. The menu features coastal cuisine, incorporating an innovative selection of fresh seafood with both international and New American culinary influences. The raw bar's stocked with juicy oysters, clams, shrimp, crab claws, and more. Consider teppan-seared jumbo sea scallops or lobster chive dumplings as an appetizer. All of the entrées are tempting: from crisp filo baked salmon to spit-roasted

## RESORT TO RESORT

If you're staying in one resort and dining in another, you need to plan ahead—even if the resorts are linked by monorail or water taxi. Why? The transportation may be operating before dinner, but if you're out late enough you'll have to get yourself home another way.

The good news is you will never be stranded. Bus transportation runs until 2 A.M.—but it's not direct. If the theme parks are closed, you'll have to take a bus to Downtown Disney and transfer to a bus that's headed to your hotel. If the theme parks are open, you can take a bus to any park and transfer to one that's headed to your resort. Keep in mind that the trip can take up to 90 minutes in either direction. If that thought is unpleasant, do what we do: take a cab. Cabs should run between about $7 and $22, depending on the destination. If you have more than three people in the party, request a van. Ask the lobby concierge.

swordfish to bluezoo's dancing fish.

Not in the mood for a selection from the sea? Consider oven-roasted filet of beef (with wild mushroom short rib ragout and bacon-wrapped asparagus) and roasted breast of chicken with lemon risotto and buttered broccolini. If you've got room when the dessert menu arrives, expect to be tempted by caramel pecan espresso cake, lime-glazed coconut cream tarts, warm chocolate cake, and more. Reservations are suggested. Note that it's possible to get food service at the bar, a plus for small groups or solo diners.

## Picabu

**B L D S** **$-$$**

A combination cafeteria and convenience store, this recently-refurbished Dolphin spot serves sandwiches, salads, burgers, pizza, and more. The checkerboard motif and jukebox raise this cafeteria atmosphere slightly above the norm. The line builds up at mealtime but moves quickly. There is ample seating. The adjoining convenience store offers snacks and sundries. The house coffee is Starbucks.

# WILDERNESS LODGE

## Artist Point

**D** **$$$-$$$$** 🐭

The Pacific Northwest theme of this restaurant is announced in landscape murals, while tall red-framed windows look out to Bay Lake. The cavernous dining room is by no means intimate, but it's not without charm.

Artist Point's hallmark is its knack for translating fresh seasonal ingredients from the Pacific Northwest into flavorful creations. An excellent example is the salmon marinated in maple whiskey, then roasted with apples and herbs and served on a smoking cedar plank. The menu may include beef, veal, buffalo, venison, and chicken selections. If the signature tomato salad is in season, please give it a try. It's available as an appetizer or a main course. The wine list features vintages, including some of the best pinot noirs, from Oregon and Washington State.

The desserts are worth making room for, no matter how full you think you are; it's just the fork-licking finale you'd expect from a restaurant of this caliber. Many guests swear by the berry cobbler, which is far from the traditional. Ask your server for a description. The cumulative effect here is an artist's palette for the sophisticated palate. Reservations are strongly suggested.

### Roaring Fork Snacks
B L D S  $  🐭

Set in a stone-walled area (a bit dungeon-like, but in an appealing way), this elaborate snack bar serves salads, burgers, fries, sandwiches, yogurt, chili, and snacks. Soft drinks, beer, and wine are also available. Sadly, it's no longer open 24 hours a day.

## ARCTIC ALERT

It's hard to imagine needing a sweater during the steamiest months of a Florida summer—but you will. Some WDW spots crank up the AC year-round. Among the shiver-inducing locales: California Grill, Mama Melrose's Ristorante Italiano, Rainforest Cafe, Jellyrolls, Atlantic Dance, and the Hoop-Dee-Doo Musical Revue (where we've actually seen chilly guests wrap themselves in tablecloths). Take our advice and plan ahead.

## ☕ Whispering Canyon Cafe
**B L D** | **$$$** | ❤

The name is ironic, as there is nothing quiet about this place. A family favorite, Whispering Canyon is one of the most boisterous Disney restaurants. All meals are offered à la carte and family style. (Family style means shared platters keep coming to the table until you say "when.")

Starting at the crack of dawn, the air is filled with aromas of bacon, sausage, and scrambled eggs. Lunch introduces sandwiches, salads, and a dessert board. For supper, expect such items as roast chicken, smoked pork ribs, and pulled pork that are sure to satisfy. Reservations are suggested.

# YACHT & BEACH CLUB

## 🏃 Beach Club Marketplace
**B L D S** | **$-$$** | ❤

The beachy setting extends to this newly redesigned space. In addition to freshly prepared menu items, there is packaged food and "grab and go" selections—salads, sandwiches, cheese and fruit plates, baked goods, gelato, and more. There is limited seating. This spot is the closest thing to a resort snack bar that you'll find in these parts. If you buy a refillable mug, this is the place to fill 'er up.

## ☕ Beaches and Cream Soda Shop
**L D S** | **$**

This classic American soda fountain is situated poolside, on the Yacht Club side of the resort. From late morning until late evening it serves up grilled burgers, chili dogs,

grilled cheese, grilled prime rib subs, and chicken caesar salad—not to mention ice cream sundaes, floats, shakes, malts, and sodas.

## 🍽 Cape May Cafe
**B D** $$-$$$ 💙

Goofy and his pals greet hungry Beach Club visitors each morning at this whimsical, beach-umbrella-decked dining area. The unlimited breakfast buffet includes all the usual breakfast standards, plus a few specialties of the house. The breakfast doesn't disappoint, but dinner is the big event here.

Dinner is presented as an all-you-can-eat New England–style clambake buffet, and it is one of the most popular meals and best overall values (though the all-inclusive price did go up a bit recently). The tempting lineup includes mussels, fish, clams, oysters, peel-and-eat shrimp, corn-on-the-cob, ribs, red-skin potatoes, chowders, and salads. If you like, dessert can be milk and cookies. Soft drinks are included. Cocktails are available at an extra charge. Reservations are suggested.

### JUST FOR GOLFERS

If you plan on playing on the Eagle Pines or Osprey Ridge courses, know that Disney's Bonnet Creek Golf Club has a pleasant dining option just for you. It's called Sand Trap Bar & Grill (💙) and it's open for three meals a day.

In addition to traditional breakfast items, Sand Trap offers appetizers, soups, and sandwiches. Ice cream and milk shakes are an option, too—as is a cocktail from the bar, where all manner of spirits can cap off a day of birdies and bogeys.

### 🏊 Hurricane Hanna's Grill
**L S** **$** 🐭

You can get hot dogs, burgers, salads, sandwiches, ice cream, and soft drinks at this poolside snack spot. There is a full bar.

### 🍽 Yacht Club Galley
**B L D** **$$-$$$** 🐭

Vivid ceramic-tile tabletops emphasize the nautical theme at the Yacht Club. Breakfast features a buffet and a full menu; lunch and dinner are à la carte. Reservations are suggested.

### 🍽 Yachtsman Steakhouse
**D** **$$$-$$$$** 🐭

You know you're in for a serious steak experience the moment you walk through the door: there's an actual butcher shop, complete with aging meats in the foyer. Elevated expectations? Maybe. But we've found that the Yachtsman consistently delivers a dining experience to rival some of the most revered steak houses of New York.

The generous portions begin with massive rolls and may continue with the spicy fried onion skillet and Yukon Gold mashed potatoes. Of course, there's no skimping on the excellent and expertly prepared aged beef entrées (prime rib, filet mignon, and chateaubriand, to name a few), so good luck finding room for crème brûlée. The menu also includes chicken and seafood dishes. As is common for the steak house milieu, the decor takes a backseat to the food. That said, the dining area is pleasant, with some secluded nooks suited for special occasions. Reservations are suggested.

# WDW DINNER SHOWS

**A** t Disney World, the name of the game is entertainment, so why should dinner be any different? In addition to venues where entertainment comes as a complimentary side dish (Biergarten in Epcot, Cosmic Ray's in the Magic Kingdom, Sci-Fi Dine-In Theater in the Disney-MGM Studios, to name just a few), there are three honest-to-goodness dinner shows to choose from. Given their popularity and longevity (the Hoop-Dee-Doo's been packing houses for three decades), there's plenty of reason to plan ahead and book "dinner as event."

## Hoop-Dee-Doo Musical Revue (Fort Wilderness) 🐭

This family favorite opened in 1974, and it's been going like gangbusters ever since. Every show begins with the stagecoach arrival of a troupe of singers and dancers who proceed to race toward the stage at Fort Wilderness resort's Pioneer Hall. What follows is 105 minutes of whoopin', hollerin', singing, dancing, and audience participation in a frontier celebration. This being a dinner show, the entertainment comes with unlimited country vittles: ribs, fried chicken (if it comes cold, we request that it be warmed up), salad, corn, and strawberry shortcake. Soft drinks, wine, and beer are included.

The gags are groaners, but the audience eats 'em up. It's all in the course of an evening at the Hoop-Dee-Doo Musical Revue, presented nightly at 5 P.M., 7:15 P.M., and 9:30 P.M. Cost is $50.92 per adult and $25.43 for children (ages 3 through 9). Prices include tax and gratuity. Reservations are necessary.

The show is presented at Pioneer Hall at Fort Wilderness year-round. It's not the easiest place in the World to get to, so allow plenty of extra travel time.

Note that the dining room is chilly, especially in the summer. Bring a sweater to combat the intense air-conditioning.

## Mickey's Backyard Barbecue (Fort Wilderness) 🐭

It's called a barbecue, but it feels like a country picnic/party, complete with a live band, games for kids, food, and Disney characters.

Presented at an open-air pavilion at Fort Wilderness, the festivities begin with music by a country band. Guests need little coaxing to get out on the floor to kick up their

heels (the dance lessons help, too), and
Disney characters join in the fun.

Dinner consists of picnic favorites:
barbecued ribs and chicken, corn-on-the-
cob, and baked beans. Beer, wine, and soft
drinks are included.

It goes without saying that kids love it,
but many couples appreciate it as an entertaining and unique Disney night out (somehow, line dancing with Goofy has a universal
appeal). For big groups, it's a full-out party.
The show is presented seasonally. Call 407-
939-3463 for a schedule and to purchase
tickets. The cost is $39.01 per adult and $25
for children ages 3 to 9.

## Hot Tip

*Though outdoors, the Spirit of Aloha and
Mickey's Backyard Barbecue are shel-
tered and presented "rain or shine"—but
the former may be canceled if the temperature drops below 50 degrees.*

### The Spirit of Aloha
### (Polynesian Resort) 🐭

A decidedly Disney luau show, the Spirit
of Aloha invites guests to participate in a
"traditional" island musical celebration. Set in
the beachfront backyard of a Hawaiian house
(at the Polynesian resort), the experience combines traditional music with more contemporary ditties from the animated Disney film
*Lilo and Stitch*. The show, complete with hula
skirts, ukuleles, and fire walkers, takes guests
on a whirlwind journey from New Zealand to
Samoa. It all stems from a (scripted and
hokey) premise about a family member who's
moved to the mainland and has lost touch
with her roots. A planned visit from said

family member prompts a gathering meant to stir up happy memories of island life.

Presented in an open-air dining theater in Luau Cove, adjacent to the Seven Seas Lagoon, the all-you-can-eat feast is influenced by the flavors of Polynesia. Menu items include roasted chicken, wild rice, and vegetables. The kids' menu features PB&J sandwiches, mac and cheese, chicken nuggets, and hot dogs. Beer, wine, soft drinks, and dessert are included. Cost is $50.22 for adults and $25.43 for kids ages 3 to 9. Prices include tax and gratuity and are subject to change.

Plan to arrive about 30 minutes before showtime, and allow extra time for transportation and parking. The show may be canceled due to inclement weather.

Reservations are necessary for this and other Disney dinner shows.

## BOOKING DINNER SHOWS

Arrangements for dinner shows may be made up to six months in advance by calling 407-WDW-DINE (939-3463). Groups of eight or more should call 407-939-7707.

A credit card number is required for all dinner show reservations. Also, it's very important to remember that cancelations for any dinner shows must be made at least 48 hours prior to showtime to avoid paying full price.

To make reservations for Walt Disney World restaurants, dial 407-WDW-DINE (939-3463). The dinner shows are quite popular, so reserve as soon as possible.

# WDW Clubs and Lounges

**W**hat distinguishes Walt Disney World clubs and lounges from many bars in the real world? Well, in addition to over-the-top theming, you can almost always get a savory nibble to accompany that cocktail. Most WDW lounges serve food, be it from their own menu, or from that of a neighboring restaurant. Hours vary according to venue, but the hot spots at Downtown Disney are usually hopping into the wee hours of the morning.

# Theme Parks

WDW CLUBS & LOUNGES

# ANIMAL KINGDOM

### Dawa Bar
A thatched roof provides shade, while the sounds of African music (occasionally live) fill the air. A full bar, including safari Amber beer, is available. It is beside the Tusker House restaurant in Harambe.

### Rainforest Cafe
The colorful Magic Mushroom bar serves, among other things, fruit blends and specialty drinks. Bar stools resemble animal legs (hooves and all). The watering hole is attached to Rainforest Cafe. Admission to the Animal Kingdom is not necessary to enter. It's possible to order from the restaurant's menu, too (see page 62).

# EPCOT

### Matsu No Ma
In addition to exotic sake-based specialty drinks, this Japan pavilion establishment offers a fine panoramic view over the whole of Epcot—including the World Showcase Lagoon, with Spaceship Earth as a back-drop—one of the best vistas of the property available (which compensates for the drab interior). Japanese beer, green tea, and cocktails are served. Sushi, sashimi, and teriyaki dishes are available.

### Rose & Crown Pub

This watering hole—a veritable symphony of polished woods, brass, and etched glass—adjoins the Rose & Crown Dining Room in the United Kingdom pavilion. British, Scottish, and Irish beers are available, along with a score of specialty drinks and appetizing snacks imported from the other side of the Atlantic. On special occasions, there may be live (and lively) piano music (see page 44).

### Sommerfest

Just outside the Biergarten restaurant in Germany, there's a shaded spot where soft pretzels, bratwurst, Black Forest cake, beer, and German wine are available.

# DISNEY-MGM STUDIOS

### Tune-In Lounge

A sitcom living room setting, with comfy couches and chairs, characterizes this lounge next to the 50's Prime Time Cafe. Waiters play the roles of sitcom "dads," and old TV sets play scenes from beloved sitcoms (all of which feature food). A full bar is available. Appetizers and entrées may be ordered from the attached restaurant (see page 52).

## NO PROOF NECESSARY

Soft drinks, fruit juices, and specialty drinks *sans* alcohol are available at all Walt Disney World bars and lounges. Just ask the bartender.

# Resorts

## ALL-STARS

### Pool Bars

In All-Star Movies, All-Star Music, and All-Star Sports there are small poolside oases: Silver Screen Spirits, Singing Spirits, and Team Spirits, respectively. Each serves a selection of beer, wine, traditional cocktails, and specialty drinks.

## ANIMAL KINGDOM LODGE

### Capetown Lounge and Wine Bar

A small lounge area within Jiko—The Cooking Place, this spot offers a selection of African wines and other spirited beverages. Guests may order from Jiko's menu (see page 77).

### Uzima Springs

A poolside bar, this small spot serves drinks and snacks during pool hours.

## DID YOU KNOW?

At Epcot's Rose & Crown Pub (located in the United Kingdom pavilion at World Showcase) a specially designed ale warmer can heat your Guinness to 55 degrees—the temperature favored by many authentic British pubs.

## Victoria Falls

An eye-popping, mezzanine-level lounge, overlooking Boma—Flavors of Africa and a small waterfall, this bar serves beer and wine with African influences, as well as cocktails, soft drinks, coffee, and tea.

# BOARDWALK

### Atlantic Dance

This dance hall showcases music (and videos) from the 1970s, '80s, and '90s. There's a full bar and a selection of specialty drinks.

### Belle Vue Room ❤

Snacks and a full bar accompany old-time tunes from antique radios in this cozy lounge. Board games are available for on-site use. (The Disney Dining plan may be redeemed for continental breakfast.)

### Big River Grille & Brewing Works

A working brewpub, this is where patrons may order appetizers at the bar and sample the brewmaster's flagship ales and specialty beers (see page 78).

### ESPN Club

The ultimate sports bar provides live broadcasts along with a menu of ballpark favorites. Occasional trivia contests (with prizes) invite participation by patrons. It's a sports fan's dream come true (see page 79).

### Jellyrolls

Dueling pianos and lively sing-alongs are the draw at this unique club, serving beer and other drinks. There is usually a cover charge of about $7 to $10. The piano players encourage requests. Don't forget to make the tip jar happy. Jellyrolls appeals to all ages.

### Leaping Horse Libation

The pool bar offers cocktails, tuna sandwiches, fruit salad, and garden salads in a carnival setting.

# CARIBBEAN BEACH

### Banana Cabana

Refreshing drinks and snack items are served at this poolside bar.

# CONTEMPORARY

### California Grill Lounge

Prime 15th-story digs are eye level to the Magic Kingdom fireworks. A selection of California wine, all manner of other drinks, and items from the restaurant menu are offered in this tiny space within the California Grill restaurant. This lounge seems to shrink more each time we visit, but it's still worth a trip (see page 82).

### Outer Rim

This lounge overlooking Bay Lake serves cocktails and appetizers after 4 P.M. The place fancies itself a sports bar, but it's not wired for premium cable, so the viewing options are limited. Still, it is an enjoyable spot for sports fans to bond. There's lots of seating and a great view of Bay Lake.

### Sand Bar

A full bar is offered poolside, weather permitting. The frozen piña coladas are certainly something to write home about. Fast food in the form of burgers, sandwiches, and salads is available at the adjacent counter area. There are shaded tables nearby.

# CORONADO SPRINGS

### Francisco's
Located in the main building, this brightly lit lounge serves specialty drinks, beer, wine, and light Mexican snacks.

### Siesta's ❤
Swimmers can take time out for burgers, sandwiches, tacos, and cocktails at this spot near the pool in the Dig Site area.

# FORT WILDERNESS

### Crockett's Tavern
Cocktails, beer, wine, wings, nachos, pizza, and light sandwiches are served in a rustic setting. The tavern is inside the Trail's End Restaurant.

# GRAND FLORIDIAN

### Garden View
A view of the pool and garden area makes this lounge a pleasant place to meet for a drink or dessert. Traditional afternoon tea is also served each day. Reservations are suggested for tea. Note that the tea experience isn't meant to be rushed. Allow time to sip slowly. And come hungry, as you'll be tempted with sandwiches and sweets.

### Mizner's
Named after the eccentric architect who defined much of the flavor of southeastern Florida's Gold Coast, this handsome retreat is on the second floor of the main building. Ports, brandies, beer, wine, cocktails, and

appetizers are featured. The atmosphere is a bit subdued in the early evening but can be raucous as the hours wear on.

### Narcoossee's

This lagoonside bar-within-a-restaurant offers international wines, as well as beer, coffee drinks, and other cocktails. It's nice to enjoy a drink on the veranda overlooking the Seven Seas Lagoon (see page 89).

### Pool Bar

A good standby with beer, frozen drinks, and fast-food items.

# DISNEY'S OLD KEY WEST

### Gurgling Suitcase

This pocket-size lounge on the Turtle Krawl boardwalk serves Key West specialties along with traditional cocktails, beer, and wine.

### Turtle Shack

Refreshments at this poolside spot include drinks and fast-food items.

# POLYNESIAN

### Barefoot Bar

An oasis next to the swimming pool, it serves beer, frozen drinks, and fast food. Item of note: frozen strawberry daquiri. (We like it mixed with the piña colada.)

### Tambu Lounge

Adjoining 'Ohana restaurant, this small tiki bar offers appetizers, specialty drinks, and traditional cocktails in a tropical setting.

There is a big-screen TV, but the view out the window is much more compelling. (Is that a volcano?)

# POP CENTURY

### Classic Concoctions
Toast the pop culture glories of yesteryear in this austere lounge, located in **Everything Pop!** Just to the left of the food court, it has ample seating for revelers. Food may be brought in, but there's no table service.

### Petals
A poolside spot serving such specialties as the "Boogie Down Margarita" and "Out-of-Sight Strawberry Daquiris."

# PORT ORLEANS FRENCH QUARTER

### Mardi Grogs
Beer, specialty drinks, and snack items are among the offerings at this poolside spot.

### Scat Cats
A New Orleans–style jazz lounge offering specialty drinks, appetizers, and (occasional) entertainment.

# PORT ORLEANS RIVERSIDE

### Muddy Rivers
The pool bar serves beer, several specialty concoctions, and fast-food items.

### River Roost

Situated in a room designed as a cotton exchange, this lounge features specialty drinks, as well as light hors d'oeuvres.

# SWAN & DOLPHIN

### Cabana Bar & Grill

Beer, frozen drinks, and fast-food selections are the main offerings at this Dolphin poolside spot.

### Copa Banana

The tabletops in this Dolphin bar resemble oversize slices of fruit, and giant pineapples and palm trees offer a fitting backdrop for tempting tropical libations, as well as more traditional cocktails.

### Kimono's

This Swan spot has a full bar, as well as sushi and other tempting treats. By night, it's a karaoke bar. Though big with the convention set, a good time is generally had by all. Come early to get a seat.

---

## GOT i.D.?

The legal drinking age in the state of Florida is 21. However, being 21 isn't enough to get served—you have to prove it. To do so, present a government-issued photo ID. If your driver's license doesn't have a photo, bring it *and* an official photo ID (a passport is ideal). Otherwise, you'll have to stick to soft drinks.

---

## Lobby Court

The winding corridors of the Swan lobby have comfortable couches and chairs, punctuated by pianos where musicians often perform. A menu with international wines, ports, and cognacs is offered seasonally.

## Shula's Steak House Lounge

The Dolphin's cozy cigar bar (in Shula's Steak House) features rich wood tones and leather chairs—the perfect place to sip a cocktail while playing armchair quarterback.

## Splash Grill

Beer, frozen drinks, and fast food are served at this Swan poolside cafe.

# WILDERNESS LODGE

## Territory Lounge

Located near Artist Point, this homage to explorers of the Old West is a nice spot for a predinner treat. Appetizers, beer, wine, and specialty drinks are served. It's possible to order food from the Artist Point menu (see page 104).

## Trout Pass

This poolside bar serves beer, frozen drinks, and snacks.

# YACHT & BEACH CLUB

## Ale and Compass

The tiny-but-charming lobby watering hole proffers a specialty-drink menu (we recommend the Bloody Marys), complete with non-Nescafé coffees. Appetizers are served, as is a continental breakfast.

### Crew's Cup

Styled after a traditional New England waterfront pub, this inviting lounge has a seafaring feel to it. It's next door to the Yachtsman Steakhouse, has almost forty beers, and is a choice spot for a drink. There is an appealing appetizer menu, too.

### Hurricane Hanna's Grill

This poolside spot, located near Stormalong Bay between the Yacht Club and Beach Club, offers specialty beverages, frozen drinks, and beer, as well as fast-food items.

### Martha's Vineyard

While a full bar is available, wines from Martha's Vineyard (and other areas) are this spot's specialty. Appetizers are served.

# Downtown Disney

### Adventurer's Club
### (Pleasure Island)

Something of an enigma, this eccentric parlor takes after the salons of the 19th-century explorers' clubs. It's decked out with photos, souvenirs, and furnishings that document the travels of its members. Silly hijinks abound. No food is served, but there's a full bar.

### BET Soundstage Club
### (Pleasure Island)

Featuring R&B, hip-hop, and house music, this urban den is reserved for patrons 21 and older (which you'll be asked to prove with a government-issued photo ID). A deejay works to keep the dance floor full all night long.

Beer, wine, and cocktails are available. Food is not. Admission is necessary.

### Bongos Cuban Cafe (West Side)

Housed inside a three-story pineapple is one of the more popular cocktail spots at Walt Disney World. There are booths and bar stools. It's possible to order food from the restaurant menu (see page 66).

### Cap'n Jack's Restaurant (Marketplace)

Agleam with copper and right on the water, this bar's specialty is its strawberry margaritas. The nibbles of garlic oysters and clam chowder on the appetizer menu are great for a snack or a meal (see page 66).

### Comedy Warehouse (Pleasure Island)

The only comedy club on WDW property, this place aspires to knock you off your bar stool with uproarious laughter. It features a group of improv comedians who field suggestions from the audience with zany results. Beer, wine, and cocktails are served, as is popcorn. Admission is necessary and is on a first-come, first-served basis. Check at the information booth (outside the club) for schedules.

### 8TRAX (Pleasure Island)

Nostalgically named for the technology of yesteryear, this spot conjures up sights and sounds of the 1970s and 1980s on a nightly basis. The only refreshments here are of the liquid variety. Admission is required.

### House of Blues (West Side)

While there is an actual bar at the back of the restaurant, it's also possible to have drinks in the enclosed Voodoo Garden (table

## PORTABLE POTABLES

It's fun to club-hop at Pleasure Island, but you can't do it with a glass in your hand. Most places are sympathetic and keep a stack of plastic cups near the door. Or plan ahead, and request that your last drink be served in plastic.

service only). Guests may order from the restaurant menu, too (see page 69).

### Mannequins (Pleasure Island)

A rotating dance floor, flashing strobe lights, and pulsating house music add up to a very popular nightspot. Restricted to guests 21 and older, Mannequins serves soft drinks and cocktails, but no snacks. There is an admission charge.

### Motion (Pleasure Island)

An enormous warehouse with a sprawling dance floor and a large bar. Admission is required.

### Raglan Road (Pleasure Island)

Top o' the evenin' to you! This establishment simply oozes Irish charm. Stop in for a pint and a live music chaser. Guests may sit at tables (and order food) or by the bar. There is no admission charge. Slainte! (That's Gaelic for "cheers.")

### Rock and Roll Beach Club (Pleasure Island)

Live music (think "Y.M.C.A.," "Shout," and "The Macarena") keeps guests dancing at this club with a surf-style influence. There is a charge to enter the club.

# Disney Dining Plan

To some, it may sound too good to be true: enjoy the convenience of pre-paid meals and stretch your vacation dollar up to 30 percent in the process. But the Disney Dining plan is just that—a package "add-on" that lets guests redeem meal vouchers at more than 100 on-property eateries and, by doing so, actually save a few bucks. The plan is flexible, too. Feeling famished? Have an extra snack or a whole meal today and skip one tomorrow. Want to be waited on hand and foot all day? Throw caution to the wind and cash in three table-service meals. Of course, that means you'll have an abundance of quick-service experiences in your future, but who cares? You're on vacation. Do what makes you happy. To learn more about the Disney Dining Plan, turn the page.

The Dining Plan is available to any guest staying at any resort that's owned and operated by Walt Disney World. (That means all resorts on WDW property, with the exception of the Swan, Dolphin, Buena Vista Palace, Best Western Lake Buena Vista, Doubletree Guest Suites, Grosvenor, Hilton, Holiday Inn, and Hotel Royal Plaza.) The plan, which starts at about $38 a day for adults, must be purchased at the same time the resort is booked. Together, the room and the dining plan are known as the "Magic Your Way Plus Dining" package. Here's what's included in the Dining Plan:

• One "Table Service" meal per person per night of their package stay.
• One "Quick Service" meal per person per night of the package.
• One snack per person, per night of their stay.

In other words, if you are booked for 6 nights at, say, the Polynesian or any other Disney owned-and-operated resort, you're entitled to 6 table-service meals, 6 quick service meals, and 6 snacks during your stay.

**One Table Service** meal includes a single serving of juice (at breakfast), an appetizer (at lunch and dinner only), an entrée, and a nonalcoholic beverage, *or* one full buffet.

## Hot Tip

*Just because your meals are pre-paid, it doesn't mean they're pre-booked! Make reservations for table service restaurants by calling 407-WDW-DINE (939-3463).*

## Hot Tip

*Kids ages 3–9 are required to order from the children's menu whenever one is available.*

**One Quick Service meal** includes an entrée, dessert (lunch and dinner only), and a nonalcoholic beverage, or one complete combo meal, plus one dessert (lunch and dinner), and a single serving of a soft drink.

**One Snack** consists of any of the following:
• Frozen ice-cream novelty, Popsicle, or fruit bar
• Popcorn scoop (single-serving box)
• Single piece of whole fruit
• Single-serving bag of snacks
• 20-ounce bottle of soda or water
• Medium fountain soft drink
• 12-ounce coffee, tea, or hot chocolate
• Single serving of prepackaged milk or juice

When it comes time for a meal or a snack, be sure to present your hotel room key (aka your "key to the world" card) before ordering. That way your server will know to charge meals to your Disney Dining Plan. Tax and gratuity are included, but we always augment the tip for exceptional service.

Each time you redeem meals or snacks from the plan, your server or cashier will give you a receipt showing the remaining balance on your Dining Plan. For example, if your party of four started with 20 table-service meals and everyone in the group used one table-service meal, your receipt

# Hot Tip

*Some eateries, such as Planet Hollywood and Wolfgang Puck Café, have a surcharge for certain menu items.*

would indicate a balance of 16 table-service meals for the remainder of your stay.

Keep in mind that all meal and snack credits must be redeemed at participating Walt Disney World locations. In this book, we've indicated these establishments by placing a 🐭 by each restaurant. However, as specifics may change, we recommend visiting *www.disneyworld.com* or calling 407-WDW-DINE (939-3463) for updates.

Finally, be aware that unused meals expire at midnight on your package reservation checkout date. So, on the last day of your trip, eat like there's no tomorrow!

## SIGNATURE RESTAURANTS

The following "Signature" restaurants, dinner shows, and character dining experiences require guests to redeem *two meals* when using the Disney Dining Plan: Jiko—The Cooking Place, Flying Fish Cafe, California Grill, Hollywood Brown Derby, Hoop-Dee-Doo Musical Revue, Mickey's Backyard Barbecue, Cítricos, Narcoossee's, The Spirit of Aloha, Artist Point, Yachtsman Steakhouse, and Cinderella's Royal Table.

# WDW Recipes

**Y**our Disney dining experience doesn't have to end when your vacation does. Though sweet souvenirs molded in the image of the Mouse may prove exceptionally satisfying, there may be more substantial culinary cravings to cure. Though your dining room isn't themed like a drive-in movie theater or a fairy-tale castle, and you rarely entertain princesses or 5-foot mice, it's still possible to whip up a little Disney magic in the privacy of your own kitchen. On the pages that follow, we've included nine of Walt Disney World's most requested recipes. Just add pixie dust.

# New England Pot Roast

*Savory pot roast is one of the most popular dishes in the Magic Kingdom's Liberty Tree Tavern (page 20), where an eighteenth-century ambience prevails and dinner is served family style.*

¼ cup chopped garlic
¼ cup vegetable oil
3 pounds boneless beef shoulder
   roast
½ cup (1 stick) butter
1 cup all-purpose flour
1 cup burgundy wine
6 cups beef broth
2 cups diced carrots
2 cups diced onions
2 cups celery, cut in large chunks
2 tablespoons chopped fresh thyme

**1.** Preheat oven to 350°F.

**2.** Sauté garlic in vegetable oil in a braising pan, then brown the meat. After meat is browned, remove from pan.

**3.** Melt the butter in the same pan, then stir in flour and continue cooking until flour is lightly browned.

**4.** Stir in burgundy wine and beef broth.

**5.** Add carrots, onion, celery, and fresh thyme.

**6.** Place meat back in the pan. Cover and bake for 40 minutes to 1 hour, or until meat is tender.

Yield: 6 servings

## Chef Mickey's Breakfast Pizza

*This kid-pleasing dish is a great way to remember the good times at Chef Mickey's at Disney's Contemporary resort (page 83), where Mickey Mouse visits during breakfast and dinner.*

One 12-inch precooked pizza shell
1 cup coarsely grated cheddar cheese
½ cup coarsely grated mozzarella cheese
½ cup coarsely grated provolone cheese
2 large eggs
¼ cup heavy cream
½ teaspoon salt, or to taste
Pinch of freshly ground black pepper, or to taste

**1.** Preheat oven to 375°F. Place pizza crust on a baking sheet.

**2.** In a medium bowl, blend the cheddar, mozzarella, and provolone cheeses.

**3.** In a small bowl, with a fork, beat together the eggs and the heavy cream, and season with the salt and pepper. Add to the cheese mixture.

**4.** Immediately, to avoid clumping, transfer the cheese mixture to the pizza shell.

**5.** Bake for 10 to 12 minutes, or until the cheese mixture is set and is beginning to brown. Cut into slices; serve hot.

Yield: 6 servings

## Tonga Toast

*This decadent, deep-fried breakfast favorite has been served for more than a quarter of a century at Disney's Polynesian resort, and is now on the menu at Kona Cafe (page 92).*

1 cup sugar
2 teaspoons cinnamon
1 loaf sourdough bread (8 inches long)
2 bananas, peeled
1 quart canola oil, for frying

**1.** Mix the sugar and cinnamon with a fork until thoroughly blended; set aside.

**2.** Slice the bread into four 2-inch-thick slices.

**3.** Cut each banana in half crosswise, then cut each piece lengthwise.

**4.** Place a bread slice flat on the counter and tear out just enough from the middle (do not tear all the way through) to stuff half a banana into it; repeat with each slice of bread.

**5.** In a large pot or a deep fryer, heat the oil to 350°F; use a candy thermometer to make certain the oil does not get any hotter, or it will burn.

**6.** Gently place one bread slice into the oil for 1 minute, or until lightly browned.

**7.** Turn and fry for another minute on the other side.

**8.** Remove bread from the deep fryer and toss it in the sugar and cinnamon mixture. Repeat for each piece.

Yield: 4 servings

# Twinkie Tiramisu

*The Pop Century resort's Everything Pop!*
*(page 94) is the place to savor this tongue-*
*in-cheek version of the classic treat.*

12 Twinkies, sliced ½ inch thick
Cocoa powder, for garnish

### Espresso Syrup
⅓ cup water
½ cup sugar
⅔ cup strongly brewed espresso coffee
¼ cup brandy (optional)

**1.** Combine water and sugar in a saucepan.

**2.** Bring to a simmer, stirring occasionally to dissolve sugar. Remove from heat, cool, and add coffee and the brandy, if using.

### Mascarpone Filling
1½ cups heavy whipping cream
⅓ cup sugar
2 teaspoons vanilla extract
1 pound mascarpone cheese,
    at room temperature

**1.** Whip cream with sugar and vanilla until soft peaks form. Fold cream into mascarpone.

**To assemble tiramisu:**

**1.** Line the bottom of a shallow 2-quart baking or gratin dish with half of the Twinkie slices.

**2.** Drizzle with half of the Espresso Syrup.

**3.** Spread with half of the Mascarpone Filling.

**4.** Repeat steps 1–3 with remaining ingredients.

**5.** Smooth the top with a metal spatula.

**6.** Cover with plastic wrap and refrigerate for up to 24 hours before serving. Sift cocoa to lightly dust the top of the tiramisu.

Yield: 8 to 10 servings

# New England Clam Chowder

*On a visit to Cape May, New Jersey, the chef collected this original recipe for "white" clam chowder served at Cape May Cafe at Disney's Beach Club resort (page 107). The creamy soup is a popular starter at the restaurant's nightly New England clambake.*

½ cup (1 stick) butter
⅓ cup all-purpose flour
2 tablespoons vegetable oil
1 large onion, finely chopped
3 stalks celery, finely chopped
2 cups clam broth
3 medium-sized red potatoes, diced into
   ½-inch pieces (about 3 cups)
2 cans (6½ ounces each) chopped
   clams, liquid reserved
1 teaspoon dried thyme leaves, crumbled
½ teaspoon dried basil leaves, crumbled
½ teaspoon salt, or to taste
¼ teaspoon freshly ground pepper, or
   to taste
4 drops Tabasco sauce, or to taste
2 cups half-and-half

**1.** Melt butter in a 2-quart saucepan over medium heat. Add flour and cook, stirring constantly, for 3 minutes. Remove the saucepan from the heat and set aside.

**2.** Heat oil in a 4- to 5-quart Dutch oven over medium heat until hot but not smoking. Add chopped onion and celery and cook, stirring, about 5 minutes, or until the onion is softened.

**3.** Stir in the clam broth, potatoes, chopped clams with their liquid, thyme, basil, salt, pepper, and Tabasco sauce. Bring the mixture to a simmer over medium heat and simmer for 5 minutes, or until the potatoes are cooked through.

**4.** Add the half-and-half and bring to a low boil over medium-high heat. Slowly add the flour mixture, whisking constantly, until well blended. Reduce the heat to low and simmer for 10 minutes, stirring occasionally.

Yield: Serves 8 as a first course or 4 as a main course (2 quarts)

# Crab and Artichoke Cakes

*Though it isn't always on the menu, this decadently rich appetizer gets raves at Victoria and Albert's, at Disney's Grand Floridian Resort & Spa (page 90).*

1 cup diced artichoke bottoms (canned or
     frozen)
1 pound lump crabmeat
¾ cup panko bread crumbs
1 teaspoon finely chopped red onion
½ teaspoon chopped fresh herbs
     (parsley, thyme, and chives)
½ cup mayonnaise
1 egg yolk
1 teaspoon Dijon mustard
1 teaspoon Worcestershire sauce
½ teaspoon Tabasco sauce
Coarse salt, to taste
Freshly ground black pepper, to taste
¼ cup (½ stick) unsalted butter

**1.** In a mixing bowl, combine artichokes, crabmeat, bread crumbs, onion, and herbs.

**2.** Add the mayonnaise, egg yolk, mustard, Worcestershire sauce, Tabasco, salt, and pepper. Mix thoroughly. Divide mixture into 8 large or 16 small crab cakes.

**3.** Heat butter in a hot sauté pan. Fry cakes till golden brown on each side. Serve immediately.

**Note:** Panko bread crumbs are coarser than those normally used in the United States and create a crunchier crust. They are sold in Asian markets.

Yield: 8 servings

## Steak Marinade

*This sweet-and-salty combination of flavors—with a generous cup of bourbon—enhances the tenderness and flavor of steaks—like those served at the Yacht Club's Yachtsman Steakhouse (page 108).*

¾ cup packed brown sugar
1 cup Jack Daniel's Tennessee Whiskey
1 cup pineapple juice
⅔ cup soy sauce
4 cups water

**1.** Combine brown sugar and Jack Daniel's in a bowl, stirring until sugar is dissolved.
**2.** Add pineapple juice and stir.
**3.** Add soy sauce and stir. Add water.
**4.** Place steaks in a 9-inch by 13-inch baking pan; pour marinade over steaks and let sit at least 24 hours in refrigerator.
**5.** Grill steaks to desired degree of doneness.

**Notes:** Marinate meat or fish for only the recommended amount of time. Over-marinating will not enhance the flavor but can cause the meat or fish to "cook" without heat, and will dehydrate and toughen it.

Cook over indirect heat. The brown sugar and soy in this marinade will cause charring when cooked over direct heat. Flip or turn the meat for at least 2 minutes after placing on the grill to reduce sticking and tearing.

Yield: Enough marinade for 12 steaks

# Sonoma Goat Cheese Ravioli

*A signature dish at California Grill (page 82), it's been simplified here for you to re-create at home.*

1 pound soft mild goat cheese (such as Montrachet), crumbled
5½ ounces aged goat cheese, crumbled
½ cup seasoned bread crumbs
2 tablespoons store-bought basil pesto
2 teaspoons extra-virgin olive oil
2 teaspoons Roasted Garlic Puree (recipe follows)
½ teaspoon salt, or to taste
⅛ teaspoon freshly ground black pepper, or to taste
16 egg roll wrappers
1 large egg and 1 tablespoon water, for egg wash
Clear Tomato Broth (optional; recipe follows)

**1.** In a large bowl, stir together the fresh goat cheese, aged goat cheese, bread crumbs, pesto, olive oil, Roasted Garlic Puree, salt, and pepper until well combined.
**2.** On a work surface, lay out 8 egg roll wrappers and brush each with the egg wash. With a sharp knife, mark each wrapper into 4 squares, taking care not to cut all the way through. Place about 1 tablespoon of the goat cheese mixture in the center of each square. Cover with the 8 remaining egg roll wrappers and press the edges together. With a knife, cut each double wrapper with filling into 4 squares, to yield 32 squares of filled ravioli. Press the edges together. (If you are not using the ravioli immediately, sprinkle lightly with cornmeal, and store refrigerated between layers of waxed paper.)

**3.** When ready to serve, cook the ravioli in a large pot of salted boiling water for 1 to 2 minutes. Drain completely. Serve with Clear Tomato Broth, if you wish.

Yield: 4 to 6 servings

### Roasted Garlic Puree

1 whole head of garlic
1 tablespoon olive oil

**1.** Preheat oven to 400°F.

**2.** Cut off the stem and top third of 1 whole garlic head. Remove peel.

**3.** Place garlic on a sheet of heavy-duty aluminum foil and drizzle with olive oil.

**4.** Wrap the garlic with foil, seal the edges tightly, and roast for 1 hour.

**5.** Remove the package from the oven, open carefully, and let the garlic cool slightly.

**6.** Scrape or squeeze out the pulp from the garlic cloves.

### Clear Tomato Broth

15 whole, vine-ripened tomatoes
1 teaspoon salt

**1.** In a blender, in batches, coarsely chop the tomatoes with salt.

**2.** Place the chopped tomatoes in a large sieve lined with a double layer of damp cheesecloth, set it over a bowl, and let the mixture drain in the refrigerator for 24 hours to collect the liquid. Discard the tomato pulp and reserve the liquid.

# Artist Point Berry Cobbler

*Artist Point at Disney's Wilderness Lodge (page 104) takes diners on a culinary journey to the Pacific Northwest with regional recipes like this berry cobbler. (It's even better with a scoop of vanilla ice cream!)*

1½ cups all-purpose flour
½ cup granulated sugar
2 teaspoons baking powder
½ teaspoon salt
½ cup (1 stick) plus 2 tablespoons cold
     butter, cut into small pieces
1 large egg
1 cup heavy cream
12 ounces fresh blueberries
2 tablespoons light brown sugar
½ pint *each* fresh raspberries and
     blackberries, and 8 strawberries

**1.** In a medium bowl, whisk together the flour, granulated sugar, baking powder, and salt. With a pastry blender, 2 knives used scissor style, or your hands, blend in ½ cup butter until crumbly. With a fork, stir in the egg and mix just enough to blend. Add heavy cream and mix just to incorporate; do not overmix.

**2.** Preheat oven to 350°F. Lightly grease a 9-inch cake pan, line the bottom with waxed paper, and grease the paper.

**3.** Press the dough evenly into the bottom of the cake pan. Place the blueberries on top of the dough and sprinkle with the brown sugar. Place the remaining butter pieces over the berries.

**4.** Bake for 20 to 25 minutes, or until golden brown. Cool on a wire rack. Remove the cake from the pan, cut in wedges, and serve with raspberries, blackberries, and strawberries.

Yield: 6 to 8 servings

# Where to Find...

**F**rom french fries to filet mignon, fried chicken to chateaubriand, Disney dishes truly run the gamut. To help you zero in on the eateries that best fit your needs, we've created a handy index of specialized lists. Once you've settled on a particular spot, flip to its entry in the book to learn more about it. And if there's a category you'd like to see but don't— tell us and we'll try to include it in next year's book.

## Bakeries/Pastry Shops

BoardWalk Bakery (BoardWalk resort)
Boulangerie Patisserie (Epcot, World Showcase)
Cinnamon Bay Bakery (Caribbean Beach resort)
Fountain View Espresso and Bakery (Epcot, Future World)
Ice Cream and Bakery Shop (Epcot, The Land)
Kringla Bakeri Og Kafe (Epcot, Norway)
Kusafiri Coffee Shop & Bakery (Animal Kingdom, Africa)
Main Street Bakery (Magic Kingdom, Main Street, U.S.A.)
Starring Rolls Cafe (Disney-MGM Studios)

## Barbecue

Flame Tree Barbecue (Animal Kingdom, DinoLand U.S.A.)
Mickey's Backyard Barbecue (*see* Dinner Shows, page 110)

## Best Bang for the Buffet Buck (all-you-can-eat)

Biergarten (Epcot, World Showcase)
Boma—Flavors of Africa (Animal Kingdom Lodge)
Cape May Cafe (Beach Club resort)
Chef Mickey's (Contemporary resort)
1900 Park Fare (Grand Floridian resort)
Trail's End Restaurant (Fort Wilderness resort)

## Best with Babies (table service)

Akershus Royal Banquet Hall (Epcot, World Showcase)
Biergarten (Epcot, World Showcase)
Chef Mickey's (Contemporary resort)
Crystal Palace (Magic Kingdom)
Donald's Breakfastosaurus (at Restaurantosaurus, in
  Animal Kingdom)
Garden Grill (Epcot, Future World)
Hollywood & Vine (Disney-MGM Studios)
'Ohana (Polynesian resort)
Olivia's Cafe (Disney's Old Key West resort)
Rainforest Cafe (Animal Kingdom and Downtown Disney)
Shutters at Old Port Royale (Caribbean Beach resort)
Tony's Town Square (Magic Kingdom, Main Street, U.S.A.)
Trail's Fnd Restaurant (Fort Wilderness resort)
Whispering Canyon Cafe (Wilderness Lodge)

INDEXES

## Brunch
House of Blues (Downtown Disney West Side)

## Buffet (all-you-can-eat)
Akershus Royal Banquet Hall (Epcot, World Showcase)
Biergarten (Epcot, World Showcase)
Boma—Flavors of Africa (Animal Kingdom Lodge)
Cape May Cafe (Beach Club resort)
Chef Mickey's (Contemporary resort)
Crystal Palace (Magic Kingdom, Main Street, U.S.A.)
Hollywood & Vine (Disney-MGM Studios)
Mickey's Backyard Barbecue (see Dinner Shows, page 110)
1900 Park Fare (Grand Floridian resort)
Spoodles (BoardWalk resort; breakfast buffet)
Trail's End Restaurant (Fort Wilderness resort)

## Burgers
Backlot Express (Disney-MGM Studios)
Cabana Bar & Grill (Dolphin resort)
Captain Cook's Snack Company (Polynesian resort)
Cosmic Ray's Starlight Cafe (Magic Kingdom, Tomorrowland)
Electric Umbrella (Epcot, Future World)
ESPN Club (BoardWalk resort)
Everything Pop! (Pop Century resort)
Food Courts (All-Star and Pop Century resorts)
Fountain, The (Dolphin resort)
Gasparilla Grill & Games (Grand Floridian resort)
Hurricane Hanna's Grill (Yacht Club resort)
Liberty Inn (Epcot, World Showcase)
McDonald's (Downtown Disney Marketplace)
Old Port Royale (Caribbean Beach resort)
Pecos Bill Cafe (Magic Kingdom, Frontierland)
Planet Hollywood (Downtown Disney, West Side)
Restaurantosaurus (Animal Kingdom, DinoLand U.S.A.)
Riverside Mill (Port Orleans Riverside resort)
Roaring Fork Snacks (Wilderness Lodge)
Sassagoula Floatworks & Food Factory (Port Orleans
   French Quarter resort)
Sci-Fi Dine-In Theater (Disney-MGM Studios)
Sunset Ranch Market (Disney-MGM Studios)

## Cheap Eats—Fast Food

Backlot Express (Disney-MGM Studios)
Casey's Corner (Magic Kingdom, Main Street, U.S.A.)
Columbia Harbour House (Magic Kingdom, Liberty Square)
Everything Pop! (Pop Century resort)
Flame Tree Barbecue (Animal Kingdom)
Harry Ramsden's Yorkshire Fish Shop (Epcot,
  World Showcase)
Restaurantosaurus (Animal Kingdom)
Sommerfest (Epcot, World Showcase)
Starring Rolls Cafe (Disney-MGM Studios)
Sunshine Seasons (Epcot, Future World)
Tusker House (Animal Kingdom)
Wolfgang Puck Express (Downtown Disney, Marketplace
  and West Side)
Yakatori House (Epcot, World Showcase)

## Cheap Eats (relatively speaking)—
## Table Service

Cap'n Jack's Restaurant (Downtown Disney, Marketplace)
Chef Mickey's (Contemporary resort)
ESPN Club (BoardWalk resort)
Olivia's Cafe (Disney's Old Key West resort)
Planet Hollywood (Downtown Disney, West Side)
Plaza Restaurant (Magic Kingdom, Main Street, U.S.A.)
Raglan Road (Downtown Disney, Marketplace)
Rainforest Cafe (Animal Kingdom and Downtown Disney,
  Marketplace)
Trail's End Restaurant (Fort Wilderness resort)

## Disney Characters (Dining with)
(*see* page 99)

## Ethnic Eateries
## African

Boma—Flavors of Africa (Animal Kingdom Lodge)
Jiko—The Cooking Place (Animal Kingdom Lodge)
Marrakesh (Epcot, World Showcase)
Tangerine Cafe (Epcot, World Showcase)

## American

Artist Point (Wilderness Lodge)
Boatwright's Dining Hall (Port Orleans Riverside resort)
California Grill (Contemporary resort)
50's Prime Time Cafe (Disney-MGM Studios)
Garden Grill (Epcot, Future World)
Grand Floridian Cafe (Grand Floridian resort)
Hollywood Brown Derby (Disney-MGM Studios)
House of Blues (Downtown Disney West Side)
Liberty Inn (Epcot, World Showcase)
Liberty Tree Tavern (Magic Kingdom, Liberty Square)
Narcoossee's (Grand Floridian resort)
1900 Park Fare (Grand Floridian resort)
Restaurantosaurus (Animal Kingdom)
Sci-Fi Dine-In Theater (Disney-MGM Studios)
Trail's End Restaurant (Fort Wilderness resort)
Yacht Club Galley (Yacht Club resort)

## British

Earl of Sandwich (Downtown Disney, Marketplace)
Harry Ramsden's Yorkshire Fish Shop (Epcot, World Showcase)
Rose & Crown Pub and Dining Room (Epcot, World Showcase)

## Canadian

Le Cellier Steakhouse (Epcot, World Showcase)

## Chinese

Lotus Blossom Cafe (Epcot, World Showcase)
Nine Dragons (Epcot, World Showcase)

## Cuban

Bongos Cuban Cafe (Downtown Disney, West Side)

## French

Bistro de Paris (Epcot, World Showcase)
Boulangerie Patisserie (Epcot, World Showcase)
Les Chefs de France (Epcot, World Showcase)

## German

Biergarten (Epcot, World Showcase)
Sommerfest (Epcot, World Showcase)

## Italian/Mediterranean

L'Originale Alfredo di Roma Ristorante (Epcot, World
   Showcase)
Mama Melrose's Ristorante Italiano (Disney-MGM Studios)
Palio (Swan resort)
Pizzafari (Animal Kingdom)
Portobello Yacht Club (Downtown Disney, Marketplace)
Spoodles (BoardWalk resort)
Tony's Town Square (Magic Kingdom, Main Street, U.S.A.)

## Japanese

Kimono's (Swan resort)
Mitsukoshi's Tempura Kiku (Epcot, World Showcase)
Mitsukoshi's Teppanyaki Dining Room (Epcot, World
   Showcase)
Yakitori House (Epcot, World Showcase)

## Mexican/Latin American

Cantina de San Angel (Epcot, World Showcase)
El Pirata y el Perico (Magic Kingdom, Adventureland)
Maya Grill (Coronado Springs resort)
San Angel Inn (Epcot, World Showcase)

## Norwegian

Akershus Royal Banquet Hall (Epcot, World Showcase)
Kringla Bakeri og Kafe (Epcot, World Showcase)

## Family-style (all-you-can-eat)

Garden Grill (Epcot, Future World)
Hoop-Dee-Doo Musical Revue (*see* page 110)
Liberty Tree Tavern (Magic Kingdom, Liberty Square)
'Ohana (Polynesian resort)
The Spirit of Aloha (*see* Dinner Shows, page 111)
Whispering Canyon Cafe (Wilderness Lodge)

## Fruit

Aloha Isle (Magic Kingdom, Adventureland)
Auntie Gravity's Galactic Goodies (Magic Kingdom,
   Tomorrowland)
Harambe Fruit Market (Animal Kingdom)

Refreshment Port (Epcot, World Showcase)
Sunset Ranch Market (Disney-MGM Studios)

## Good for Groups
Biergarten (Epcot, World Showcase)
Boma—Flavors of Africa (Animal Kingdom Lodge)
California Grill (Contemporary resort)
Crystal Palace (Magic Kingdom, Main Street, U.S.A.)
Flame Tree Barbecue (Animal Kingdom)
Hollywood & Vine (Disney-MGM Studios)
House of Blues (Downtown Disney, West Side)
Mitsukoshi's Teppanyaki Dining Room (Epcot, World
   Showcase)
Sunset Ranch Market (Disney-MGM Studios)
Sunshine Seasons (Epcot, Future World)
Wolfgang Puck Café (Downtown Disney, West Side)
Wolfgang Puck Café—The Dining Room (Downtown
   Disney, West Side)

## Hot Dogs
Backlot Express (Disney-MGM Studios)
Casey's Corner (Magic Kingdom, Main Street, U.S.A.)
Food Courts (All-Star and Pop Century resorts)
Liberty Inn (Epcot, World Showcase)
The Mara (Animal Kingdom Lodge)
Restaurantosaurus (Animal Kingdom)
Sunset Ranch Market (Disney-MGM Studios)
Wetzel's Pretzels (Downtown Disney, Marketplace and
   West Side)

## Ice Cream and Frozen Treats
Aloha Isle (Magic Kingdom, Adventureland)
Anandapur Ice Cream (Animal Kingdom)
Cool Post (Epcot, World Showcase)
Enchanted Grove (Magic Kingdom, Fantasyland)
Ghirardelli Soda Fountain and Chocolate Shop (Downtown
   Disney, Marketplace)
Min & Bill's Dockside Diner (Disney-MGM Studios)
Mrs. Potts's Cupboard (Magic Kingdom, Fantasyland)
Plaza Ice Cream Parlor (Magic Kingdom, Main Street, U.S.A.)

Plaza Restaurant (Magic Kingdom, Main Street, U.S.A.)
Scuttle's Landing (Magic Kingdom, Fantasyland)
Seashore Sweets' (BoardWalk resort)
Sleepy Hollow (Magic Kingdom, Liberty Square)
Sunshine Tree Terrace (Magic Kingdom, Adventureland)
Tamu Tamu Refreshments (Animal Kingdom)

## Kids' Favorites

Akershus Royal Banquet Hall (Epcot, World Showcase)
Captain Cook's Snack Company (Polynesian resort)
Casey's Corner (Magic Kingdom, Main Street, U.S.A.)
Chef Mickey's (Contemporary resort)
Cinderella's Royal Table (Magic Kingdom, Fantasyland)
Crystal Palace (Magic Kingdom, Main Street, U.S.A.)
50's Prime Time Cafe (Disney-MGM Studios)
Garden Grill (Epcot, Future World)
Hoop-Dee-Doo Musical Revue (see Dinner Shows,
   page 110)
Liberty Inn (Epcot, World Showcase)
1900 Park Fare (Grand Floridian resort)
Pecos Bill Cafe (Magic Kingdom, Frontierland)
Pinocchio Village Haus (Magic Kingdom, Fantasyland)
Planet Hollywood (Downtown Disney, West Side)
Rainforest Cafe (Animal Kingdom and Downtown Disney,
   Marketplace)
Restaurantosaurus (Animal Kingdom)
Sci-Fi Dine-In Theater (Disney-MGM Studios)
Sunset Ranch Market (Disney-MGM Studios)
Sunshine Seasons (Epcot, Future World)
Toy Story Pizza Planet (Disney-MGM Studios)
Whispering Canyon Cafe (Wilderness Lodge)

## Knockout Views

Big River Grille & Brewing Works (outdoor seating;
   BoardWalk resort)
California Grill (Contemporary resort)
Cantina de San Angel (Epcot, World Showcase)
Cap'n Jack's Restaurant (Downtown Disney,
   Marketplace)
Coral Reef (Epcot, Future World)
Garden Grill (Epcot, Future World)

Narcoossee's (Grand Floridian resort)
Rose & Crown Pub and Dining Room (Epcot, World Showcase)
Tomorrowland Terrace Noodle Station (Magic Kingdom,
  Tomorrowland)

## Kosher (fast-food selections)

ABC Commissary (Disney-MGM Studios)
Cosmic Ray's Starlight Cafe (Magic Kingdom, Tomorrowland)
Everything Pop! (Pop Century resort)
Food Courts (All-Star and Port Orleans Riverside resorts)
Pizzafari (Animal Kingdom)

## Lounges and Bars (with Food)

Ale and Compass (Yacht Club resort)
Banana Cabana (Caribbean Beach resort)
Barefoot Bar (Polynesian resort)
Big River Grille & Brewing Works (BoardWalk resort)
Bongo's Cuban Cafe (Downtown Disney West Side)
Cabana Bar & Grill (Dolphin resort)
California Grill Lounge (Contemporary resort)
Capetown Lounge and Wine Bar (inside Jiko—The
  Cooking Place; Animal Kingdom Lodge)
Cap'n Jack's Restaurant (Downtown Disney, Marketplace)
Captain's Tavern (Caribbean Beach resort)
Crew's Cup (Yacht Club resort)
Crocket's Tavern (Fort Wilderness resort)
ESPN Club (BoardWalk resort)
Francisco's (Coronado Springs resort)
Garden View (Grand Floridian resort)
Gurgling Suitcase (Disney's Old Key West resort)
Hurricane Hanna's Grill (Yacht & Beach Club resorts)
Kimono's (Swan resort)
Leaping Horse Libations (BoardWalk resort)
Mardi Grogs (Port Orleans French Quarter resort)
Martha's Vineyard (Beach Club resort)
Matsu No Ma (Inside Japan; Epcot, World Showcase)
Mizner's (Grand Floridian resort)
Muddy Rivers (Port Orleans Riverside resort)
Narcoossee's (Grand Floridian resort)
Outer Rim (Contemporary resort)
Portobello Yacht Club (Downtown Disney, Marketplace)

Rainforest Cafe (Magic Mushroom bar; Animal Kingdom
  and Downtown Disney, Marketplace)
Raglan Road (Downtown Disney, Pleasure Island)
River Roost (Port Orleans Riverside resort)
Rose & Crown Pub and Dining Room (Epcot, World Showcase)
Sand Bar (Contemporary resort)
Sand Trap Bar & Grill (Bonnet Creek Golf Club;
  *see* page 107)
Siesta's (Coronado Springs resort)
Sommerfest (Inside Germany; Epcot, World Showcase)
Splash Grill (Swan resort)
Stone Crab Lounge (Inside Fulton's Crab House; Downtown
  Disney, Marketplace)
Tambu (lounge; Polynesian resort)
Territory (Wilderness Lodge)
Trout Pass (Wilderness Lodge)
Tune-In Lounge (Disney-MGM Studios)
Turtle Shack (Disney's Old Key West resort)
Uzima Springs (Animal Kingdom Lodge)

## New to WDW

Raglan Road (Downtown Disney Pleasure Island)
Studios Catering Co. & Flatbread Grill (Disney-MGM Studios)
Sunshine Seasons (Epcot, Future World)
Tomorrowland Terrace Noodle Station (Magic Kingdom,
  Tomorrowland)

## Open 24 Hours

Captain Cook's Snack Company (Polynesian resort)
Gasparilla Grill & Games (Grand Floridian resort)

INDEXES

DID YOU KNOW?

The Contemporary resort's California Grill
serves about 70 pounds of tomatoes *every
night* during tomato season (July through
November).

Picabu (Dolphin resort)
Snack Bar (Contemporary resort)
Watercress Pastry Shop (Buena Vista Palace resort)

## Pizza

California Grill (Contemporary resort)
Cheesecake Factory Express (Downtown Disney, West Side)
Everything Pop! (Pop Century resort)
Food Courts (All-Star resorts)
Gasparilla Grill & Games (Grand Floridian resort)
L'Original Alfredo di Roma Ristorante (Epcot, World
  Showcase; lunch only)
Mama Melrose's Ristorante Italiano (Disney-MGM Studios)
Pinocchio Village Haus (Magic Kingdom, Fantasyland)
Pizzafari (Animal Kingdom)
Planet Hollywood (Downtown Disney, West Side)
Riverside Mill (Port Orleans Riverside resort)
Roaring Fork Snacks (Wilderness Lodge)
Royal Pizza Shop (Caribbean Beach resort)
Sassagoula Floatworks & Food Factory (Port Orleans
  French Quarter resort)
Spoodles (BoardWalk resort)
Sunset Ranch Market (Disney-MGM Studios)
Toy Story Pizza Planet (Disney-MGM Studios)
Trail's End Restaurant (Fort Wilderness resort)
Wolfgang Puck Café (Downtown Disney, West Side)
Wolfgang Puck Express (Downtown Disney, Marketplace
  and West Side)

## Salads

Artist's Palette (Saratoga Springs Resort & Spa)
Big River Grille & Brewing Works (BoardWalk resort)
Boma—Flavors of Africa (Animal Kingdom Lodge)
Cape May Cafe (Beach Club)
Chef Mickey's (Contemporary resort)
Cinderella's Royal Table (Magic Kingdom, Fantasyland)
Columbia Harbour House (Magic Kingdom, Liberty Square)
Cosmic Ray's Starlight Cafe (Magic Kingdom,
  Tomorrowland)
Crystal Palace (Magic Kingdom, Main Street, U.S.A.)
Hollywood Brown Derby (Disney-MGM Studios)

Le Cellier Steakhouse (Epcot, World Showcase)
1900 Park Fare (Grand Floridian resort)
Pecos Bill Cafe (Magic Kingdom, Frontierland)
Pepper Market (Coronado Springs resort)
Pinocchio Village Haus (Magic Kingdom, Fantasyland)
Plaza Restaurant (Magic Kingdom, Main Street, U.S.A.)
Rainforest Cafe (Animal Kingdom and Downtown Disney, Marketplace)
Sunshine Seasons (Epcot, Future World)
Tusker House (Animal Kingdom)
Wolfgang Puck Café (Downtown Disney West Side)

## Seafood

Artist Point (Wilderness Lodge)
Cape May Cafe (Beach Club)
Cap'n Jack's Restaurant (Downtown Disney, Marketplace)
Columbia Harbour House (Magic Kingdom, Liberty Square)
Coral Reef (Epcot, Future World)
Flying Fish Cafe (BoardWalk resort)
Fulton's Crab House (Downtown Disney, Marketplace)
Narcoossee's (Grand Floridian resort)
Todd English's bluezoo (Dolphin resort)

## Snack Bars (at the Resorts)

Cabana Bar & Grill (lounge; Dolphin resort)
Captain Cook's Snack Company (Polynesian resort)
Gasparilla Grill & Games (Grand Floridian resort)
Hurricane Hanna's Grill (Yacht Club)
Picabu (Dolphin resort)
Roaring Fork Snacks (Wilderness Lodge)
Sand Bar (lounge; Contemporary resort)
Snack Bar (Contemporary resort)

## Solo Diners

Cap'n Jack's Restaurant (Downtown Disney, Marketplace)
Crew's Cup (lounge, Yacht Club resort)
ESPN Club (BoardWalk resort)
Flying Fish Cafe (BoardWalk resort)
Tune-In Lounge (Disney-MGM Studios)
Wolfgang Puck Café (sushi bar; Downtown Disney, West Side)

## Steak

Le Cellier Steakhouse (Epcot, World Showcase)
Shula's Steak House (Dolphin resort)
Yachtsman Steakhouse (Yacht Club resort)

## Super Splurges (for Grown-ups)

Artist Point (Wilderness Lodge)
Bistro de Paris (Epcot, World Showcase)
California Grill (Contemporary resort)
Jiko—The Cooking Place (Animal Kingdom Lodge)
Le Chefs de France (Epcot, World Showcase)
Shula's Steak House (Dolphin resort)
Todd English's bluezoo (Dolphin resort)
Victoria & Albert's (Grand Floridian resort)
Wolfgang Puck Café and The Dining Room (Downtown
    Disney, West Side)
Yachtsman Steakhouse (Yacht Club resort)

## Sushi

California Grill (Contemporary resort)
Kimono's (lounge; Swan resort)
Mitsukoshi Tempura Kiku (Epcot, World Showcase)
Wolfgang Puck Café (Downtown Disney, West Side)
Yakitori House (Epcot, World Showcase)

## Terrific Theming

Akershus Royal Banquet Hall (Epcot, World Showcase)
Biergarten (Epcot, World Showcase)
Cinderella's Royal Table (Magic Kingdom, Fantasyland)
50's Prime Time Cafe (Disney-MGM Studios)
Liberty Tree Tavern (Magic Kingdom, Liberty Square)
'Ohana (Polynesian resort)
The Plaza (Magic Kingdom, Main Street, U.S.A.)
Rainforest Cafe (Animal Kingdom and Downtown Disney,
    Marketplace)
Sci-Fi Dine-In Theater (Disney-MGM Studios)

## Vegetarian Selections

Boma—Flavors of Africa (Animal Kingdom Lodge)
Cheesecake Factory Express (Inside DisneyQuest;

Downtown Disney, West Side)
Columbia Harbour House (Magic Kingdom, Liberty Square)
Cosmic Rays Starlight Cafe (Magic Kingdom, Tomorrowland)
Everything Pop! (Pop Century resort)
Food Courts (All-Star resorts)
L'Originale Alfredo di Roma Ristorante (Epcot, World
    Showcase)
Mama Melrose's Ristorante Italiano (Disney-MGM Studios)
Marrakesh (Epcot, World Showcase)
Pizzafari (Animal Kingdom)
Planet Hollywood (Downtown Disney, West Side)
Rainforest Cafe (Animal Kingdom and Downtown Disney,
    Marketplace)
Spoodles (BoardWalk resort)
Sunset Ranch Market (Disney-MGM Studios)
Sunshine Seasons (Epcot, Future World)
Tomorrowland Terrace Noodle Station (Magic Kingdom,
    Tomorrowland)
Tony's Town Square (Magic Kingdom, Main Street, U.S.A.)
Tusker House (Animal Kingdom)
Wolfgang Puck Express (Downtown Disney, West Side
    and Marketplace)

# Wine and Dine (great wine lists)

Artist Point (Wilderness Lodge)
Boma—Flavors of Africa (Animal Kingdom Lodge)
California Grill (Contemporary resort)
Citricos (Grand Floridian resort)
Flying Fish Cafe (BoardWalk resort)
Jiko—The Cooking Place (Animal Kingdom Lodge)
Le Chefs de France (Epcot, World Showcase)
Narcoossee's (Grand Floridian resort)
Palio (Swan resort)
Shula's Steak House (Dolphin resort)
Victoria & Albert's (Grand Floridian resort)
Wolfgang Puck Café (Downtown Disney West Side)
Wolfgang Puck Café—The Dining Room (Downtown
    Disney West Side)
Yachtsman Steakhouse (Yacht Club resort)

# Index

INDEXES